The
NETWORK
Effect

Selected Reviews

Here are a few extracts from the many testimonials that
The Network Effect has received. You'll find more on
www.TheNetworkEffect.co.uk and *www.Amazon.co.uk*

"Full of encouragement, this is the book you need to make
it happen for you."

JOHN STOPFORD, *Emeritus Professor of International Business,*
London Business School

"Now that I can show my colleagues your magnificent piece of work,
recommending you for various customized executive programmes is
a pleasure."

PATRICK FURU PhD, *Academic Director, Executive Education,*
Hanken School of Economics, Helsinki

"A timely, detailed and practical guide... an invaluable step by step
guide... A must-read for anyone wanting to get on either socially,
politically or in business."

LOUISE BURFITT-DONS, *Founder, RSAWSN (Royal Society of Arts Women*
Speaker's Network)

"Newton and Perle have distilled key insights into an eminently
readable book replete with numerous useful, well-framed vignettes
and case studies that are easy to digest and act upon. The themes run
the gamut from truisms to more complicated points. A must read for
anyone interested in enhancing and expanding their social horizons
for career or other reasons."

PETER R, *Partner, Global Partnership Forum, New York*

"The quintessential guide to networking for those who want to get
ahead in their career. The highly readable, easy to digest format...
encourages and empowers the reader to success in this essential
life-long skill."

BRIAN MARRINAN, *MBA Careers Services Manager, UCD Smurfit*
Business School, Dublin

"It's an easy read but you'll end up knowing exactly how to 'do networking'. Fabulous!"

DR PATRICK TISSINGTON, *Associate Dean, Business Partnerships, Aston Business School*

"... a really useful and readable book. It focuses on the soft skills that we often take for granted but do not always work on as we should... plenty of suggestions about how to improve networking skills and I think that I will repeatedly find myself dipping back into this practical book."

DR. PHIL HODES, *consultant psychiatrist*

"I like it when people give concrete examples of what they are talking about, and so it was good to see so many case examples."

HARVEY RATNER, *brief therapist*

"Congratulations on such an interesting book. I think you are spot on. I was fascinated to read the case studies."

CAROLE STONE, *Managing Director, YouGovStone*

"This book is for anyone who ever said, 'But I don't really like/feel comfortable/know how to network.' It's all here... Whether you're a recent graduate just starting out or a seasoned professional needing to up your game, this book provides valuable tips and ideas."

PATRICIA KEENER, *career coach*

" where this book really stands out... is the way it engages with a large amount of practical advice, real-world case studies, and encouragement to try various 'hand-on' exercises."

JOHN HAMLEN, *Operations Director, Simply Business Skills*

"An excellent roundup of proven techniques for effective networking... Perfect for those who are entering the workplace and invaluable revision for experienced networkers."

PAUL TANNER, *business/IT consultant*

"I found this book really easy to use. I flicked through and found lots of handy hints that made perfect sense and reinforced the importance of doing all those thoughtful things that I sometimes forget."

LARA MEREDITH, *University of Nottingham*

"The subject matter of this book could not be any more current and relevant. It would be great if the business schools made it required reading. It addresses issues fundamental to succeeding in business today."

SIAMAK BASHI, *Managing Director, CQout*

"Being a good communicator does not necessarily make you a good networker but this really inspired me to think about converting my skills into effective networking opportunities. This would also be a good book for young adults and those starting out on a career pathway. I highly recommend it."

ALISON BENSON, *Owner, Indigo Research*

"I learn by doing or looking at what others do and for me the most useful parts of the book were the practical examples. Even if you only read the examples and practice the networking you will still learn a lot from this book."

SHADI KELLY, *MBA Careers Director & Consultant/Faculty, Ashridge Business School*

"Networking is akin to public speaking for many people, but it won't be after they read this book. It actually takes the fear and anxiety out of the process and makes it seem easy if not even fun."

DR ELLEN PRUYNE, *change consultant*

"The fluent and intelligent narrative is deftly interspersed with skilful graphics... We are led into a world where we can successfully navigate the jungle of employment and marketing opportunities and ride the wave to success... this book is an invaluable asset."

MARGALIT HALUTZ, *Electronic Resources, Open University Library, Israel*

"There are hundreds of books on how to run a business or get ahead in the workplace but few concentrate on networking. This well-researched and enjoyable read is... a must for anyone in the world of work."

JEANNE GRIFFITHS, *writer & editor*

"Debunks the myth that networking is all about 'working a room' and exchanging business cards."

ANGELA EDKINS, *Career Adviser, Aston Business School*

"... an extremely well-written book... I had to stop myself reading too much as it was slowing down the design process!"

GUY CALLABY, *Giraffic Design*

"... an engaging and practical guide, focusing not only on establishing networks but how to nurture and sustain them. This well-thought-out book is cleverly written by people who know and have practised their subject well... Consider the time you spend with this book a shrewd and valuable investment!"

JO BROMPTON, *sales professional*

"[A] practical, easy to read... indispensable handbook for anyone whose stock in trade is building and maintaining relationships."

STEVEN LEOF, *business development*

"The experience of the authors shines through and it matters not if you are at Networking 101 level or a black belt master, there will something useful in here."

MIKE PHIPPS, *Politics At Work Ltd*

"... the case studies make the advice come alive. In addition, [the] exercises... assist the new or "reluctant" networker to get out and 'just do it'."

MARGO HAMEL, *First Vice President, SunTrust Bank*

Management Advantage Ltd
39a Brondesbury Villas
London
NW6 6AJ

Published by Management Advantage Ltd in 2011
www.ManAdvan.com

Designed by Guy Callaby www.guycallaby.co.uk

A catalogue record for this book is available from the British Library.

ISBN 978-0-9567098-0-6

Printed in Great Britain by TJ International Ltd, Padstow, Cornwall

Management
Advantage

The
NETWORK
Effect

A practical guide to
making – and keeping –
the connections that can
make your world go round

Tony Newton & Judith Perle

About the authors

Ali Baskerville

Judith Perle

Judith brings to her training work experience in business communication gained over a career in publishing, branding, marketing and new business development. She was Brand Development Director for illustrated publisher Dorling Kindersley, and Brand Liaison Director for the Superbrands organisation. Judith holds a Masters in Business Management from London Business School.

She also has over 15 years experience publishing books, magazines and partworks and has created, edited and managed consumer publications on subjects ranging from gardening to interior design. She has been involved in publishing start-ups and negotiated intellectual property licensing rights with many global publishers, including household names such as Reader's Digest, Time Life Books and HarperCollins. Judith also works with the MicroLoan Foundation (*www.MicroLoanFoundation.org.uk*), a charity which provides small loans to women entrepreneurs in Africa to help them start or develop businesses and work their way out of poverty.

Tony Newton

Tony combines a life sciences background with a Masters in Business Management from London Business School and has held senior corporate communications positions within FTSE 250 and Nasdaq 100 companies, with responsibilities covering the entire corporate communications and investor relations spectrum.

Tony's science, medicine and technology writing has appeared in *The Times*, the *Independent* and numerous lay and specialist publications. He has also broadcast for the BBC and written extensively for the web. Tony's management training role meshes with his work as co-founder and director of online marketplace CQout Ltd, and with corporate communications and copy writing activities for a number of medical device and pharma companies.

Tony is engaged in doctoral research into networking at Durham Business School.

Tony and Judith are the founders and directors of management training consultancy, Management Advantage (*www.ManAdvan.com*).

Dedication

With grateful thanks to the Sloan Fellowship at London Business School, which threw us together and provided the crucible in which a friendship and a business partnership were forged, and which took both our careers in a direction we would never have anticipated.

Thanks, too, to our clients, colleagues and, especially, workshop participants. Without your lively and critical participation, we couldn't have collected the many and varied case studies that bring the real world to what follows.

Contents

Turning 'Order Qualifiers' Into 'Order Winners'

It could be said that the first telephone was a complete waste of time: it was only when it was connected to a second telephone that two people could actually talk to each other. As more people connected to this phone network, the more important and useful joining in was perceived to be. This is what is meant in traditional business jargon as a 'network effect': the more people get involved, the greater the benefit of being involved.

But getting people to join the telephone network was never just a matter of making a watertight business or social case for it. For the idea to take off, people had to talk about it. In short, for this 'network effect' to occur, people had to communicate with each other: they had to network.

Whether we're talking about the emergence of a dominant technology, the adoption of a new fashion, the success of a new restaurant or access to crucial information about a job vacancy, research demonstrates that it is often the activity of a relatively small number of highly networked individuals that determines the outcome. The traits demonstrated by those individuals – who may themselves be unaware of exactly what makes them so influential – can be codified and taught.

Whether you're an entrepreneur, a consultant, a jobseeker, in sales or business development, or simply want to move your career in the right direction, this book will attempt to walk you through everything you need to know about connecting with other people. We can say that with certainty because it's been written as an extension of the interactive workshops that we've run for business schools, companies and other organisations since 2001.

Before we wrote even a single word, we grabbed every book on networking-related topics that we could find, and rated them subjectively on two criteria. One axis measured the extent to which they were ideas-based (i.e. 'Here's some interesting info, but what you do with it is up to you!') or actions-based (i.e. 'Do this, this and this and Bob's your uncle!'). On the other axis, we tracked the scope of each book: knowing how to 'work a room' effectively is a useful skill but it's by no means all there is to the networking process. What about building relationships, staying in touch with people, playing by the rules of the game – not to mention seemingly insignificant details like finding a way to remember people's names?

What that exercise confirmed was the need for a book that gives sound, proven and above all practical advice underpinned by an explanation of the relevant concepts. If you understand 'why' something works as well as 'how', you have a far better chance of making it work for you. And that, in the final analysis, is our aim – to turn each and every one of you into a better networker.

Business schools and professional training bodies the world over are busy following a 'hard skills' syllabus that traditionally teaches strategy, finance, marketing and the like. If you've done the Operations Management module, you might be familiar with the concept of 'order qualifiers' and 'order winners'. An 'order qualifier' is a feature of your product or service of which you might justly be very proud, but that ultimately only gets you as far as the beauty parade. The 'order winner' is that unique attribute that gets you the business, the job, the funding or the promotion.

People and businesses often mistake their 'order qualifiers' for 'order winners'. Think about it: every accountancy firm pitching for new business has nearly identical 'technical skills' in their ability to conduct an audit, for example. Every solicitor needs to be able to decipher what is actually meant by 'the party of the first part' and 'the party of the third part'. Every dentist must know how to administer a local anaesthetic. Every MBA graduate should have a decent grasp of the core syllabus.

So what is the 'order winner' in these cases? The answer is that it's often the so-called 'soft skills' that are supremely important in differentiating one candidate, proposal or service from another. It's commonly said that most business is done on the golf course, and even if that's not actually true, it most certainly is in a metaphorical sense... and it is effective networking skills that make it all possible. This book won't open doors for you, but it will give you the best possible chance of opening them for yourself.

Based on the feedback we receive from our workshops, we've made this book as practical as we know how. It's filled with tips and tricks – practical stuff that you can (and should) try out for yourself – together with masses of real-life examples and anecdotes culled from our own experience and also, perhaps more importantly, the many people we've met and taught. Without them, as they say, this book wouldn't have been possible.

All the case studies in this book are real. They have either happened to us, been witnessed by us or been reported to us. Where necessary, names have been changed to preserve anonymity.

TONY NEWTON & JUDITH PERLE
Management Advantage
www.ManAdvan.com

CHAPTER ONE

Why Develop a Networking Culture?

"When _I_ use a word," Humpty Dumpty said,
in rather a scornful tone, "it means just what
I choose it to mean – neither more nor less."

LEWIS CARROLL *Through the Looking Glass*

O pen a copy of *The Times* or the *Financial Times* appointments pages at random, and you'll often find job descriptions that include words to this effect: "Must have excellent networking skills". Occasionally, as in this ad that appeared in *The Times*, effective networking skills is the one 'must-have' attribute.

Pick up an industry conference programme and you'll typically see one if not more references to networking in the list of 'reasons to go'. To take just one example, the publicity pamphlet for the prestigious Institute of Directors 2007 Annual Convention claims that "the IoD's flagship event enables directors to learn, lobby, network and entertain" and provides an opportunity to "network with some of the most successful and influential business leaders in the UK." In 2009, the pamphlet talked about "Strong networking support. Benefit from the UK's largest gathering of CEOs, MDs, VPs, Chairmen and Directors – all under one stately roof – with pre-event networking built into this intensive one-day programme."

But what exactly is this 'networking' thing, and why is it so important? It's not a bad idea to lay some ghosts right at the outset by defining what networking is NOT, before getting on to the positives:

- Networking is not about manipulating people to get what you want

- Networking is not just about 'working a room' in order to give your business card to anyone who will take it

- Networking is not using the 'old boy' connection to get something that should rightfully have gone to someone else

- Having a membership list, alumni directory or industry database does not mean you have a network

- Networking is not selling: networking is about opening doors, keeping them open and seeing where they lead. Selling is about 'closing'. There are a lot of similarities in the techniques involved, and effective networking can undoubtedly help you make sales and win business, but if you're seen to be selling, people are likely to slam that open door in your face...hard.

Before we start looking at what networking really involves, or even attempt to define it, take a few moments to fill in the following questionnaire. It's not an exam, so just give spontaneous answers to the questions, and tot up your score before reading on.

DO TRY THIS

How Good Are Your Networking Skills?

I always know the right person to contact when I need help, advice or information.
(Not true at all)   1   2   3   4   5   (Very true)

I am at ease walking into a room full of people I have never met before (e.g. at a drinks reception or conference).
(Not true at all)   1   2   3   4   5   (Very true)

I encourage people to network with me and rarely turn down an opportunity to make a new contact.
(Not true at all)   1   2   3   4   5   (Very true)

continued overleaf

continued from previous page

I feel comfortable making important telephone calls.
(Not true at all)   1   2   3   4   5   (Very true)

I am confident of my ability to write clear and persuasive business letters.
(Not true at all)   1   2   3   4   5   (Very true)

I make an effort to introduce people I know to each other.
(Not true at all)   1   2   3   4   5   (Very true)

After meeting someone, I store their details (including general information on interests, where we met, etc.) in an easily accessible format.
(Not true at all)   1   2   3   4   5   (Very true)

I add at least one new contact to my database each week.
(Not true at all)   1   2   3   4   5   (Very true)

My database is backed up at regular, and frequent, intervals.
(Not true at all)   1   2   3   4   5   (Very true)

I make a point of keeping in touch with people on a regular basis.
(Not true at all)   1   2   3   4   5   (Very true)

Total Score _____

That wasn't too difficult, was it? If you scored highly, it shows that you're already fairly well in tune with many of the concepts and practical techniques that we'll discuss in this book. If you scored lower, it just means that the ink between these covers should be of even more use to you. In fact, we've pulled a little bit of sleight of hand on you here, because what's really interesting here is not just your total score, but the distribution. You probably scored worse on some questions than others. Which ones? Raising those scores is what you need to do to raise your networking game; we hope the following chapters will set you well on the road to doing just that.

But there was another reason for including this exercise. What do phone calls have to do with networking? Think about it for a moment:

if someone is good enough to put you in touch with a contact of theirs who might be able to help you in some way, and you start out by making a poor phone call, you may well have blown your one opportunity to make an impression. Not only that, you've possibly damaged the credibility of the kind soul who gave you the contact in the first place. Would that make them eager to help you again?

What about your contacts database – since when was that part of the networking process? Well, since written records began, actually. Being able to remember personal and work related details about people pays them a huge psychological compliment. The message it sends on a subliminal level is "what you said to me when we last met was important enough to stick in my mind", and that's a great way to get people on your side, as we'll demonstrate. But you can't possibly remember everything about everyone, so you have to write it down somewhere. That makes a good database an invaluable asset.

Look again at the questionnaire and you'll see where this is leading. The fact is that, whether it's aimed at business development, project financing, setting up a business or job-hunting, effective networking is really about optimising our skills in sending and receiving appropriate messages (and blocking inappropriate ones!) in the three ways that human beings communicate with each other for business: face to face, by phone and in writing. As with so much in life, the key thing is to make the most of our strengths while minimising our weaknesses.

IN A NUTSHELL

To network effectively, you've got to be able to communicate effectively.

Perhaps we should manage your expectations at this point. This book isn't one of the 'everything you ever need to know about X' variety. Although we firmly believe that communicating by phone and in writing are essential parts of any networking strategy, we also realise that we can't conquer the world in a single volume. So, rather than biting off more than we can chew, and either producing a mammoth book or failing to do justice to any one subject, we've decided to concentrate on face to face networking skills.

Throughout this book, we'll be giving examples of how networking has been demonstrably effective, but to set the scene and establish the importance of networking, here's a case study that shows the downside of not having an effective network.

CASE STUDY

Where Were You When I Needed You?

In a speech at London Business School, Chris Ingram, founder of the Tempus media-buying group, recalled the battle he fought to prevent WPP gaining control of the company back in 1996. He told how he needed to raise £6 million in a very short space of time. As he reported, "I couldn't do it: I just didn't have the network."

The result was that Martin Sorrell's WPP took a sizeable stake in Tempus, and by 2001 had built its holding to nearly 25%. But Ingram had learnt his lesson, had built his connections in the City and ended up selling the company after an auction between WPP and their competitor Havas.

Ultimately, WPP bought the company for £432 million at a multiple of 35 (yes, 35!), through which Ingram made £64 million for himself, but the hostile nature of the takeover led to his eventual departure from the company he had created. His analysis at the time? "I would have sneered at the need to network five years ago. I certainly don't now!"

So not having an effective network when you need it can spell trouble, if not downright disaster. Whether you're one of the top team, or just starting out in your career (or anywhere in between), you need a network to rely on. Contrast the situation you've just read about with what happens when an entrepreneur has an effective network that is easy to mobilise.

CASE STUDY

The Rich List

Richard Reed, co-founder of smoothie-maker Innocent Drinks, recalls the way in which the company got started at a local music festival: "We put out a big bin that said 'yes' and a big bin that said 'no'. Then we put a sign over our stall which said: 'Should we give up our day jobs to make these smoothies?' We asked everyone who bought our smoothies to put their empty bottles in one of the bins. Fortunately the 'yes' bin was pretty full, so that gave us the confidence to resign from our jobs the next day."

"You can start a fruit juice business with the money you've got in your pocket," says Richard. "You can go out and buy whatever fruit you can afford, then turn it into juice, then sell it and use the money to buy more fruit the next day. But when we went to start the business on a more commercial scale we obviously needed things like a refrigerator van to deliver the juices, some fridges to put the juices in...things like that required a bit of investment up front."

But how did Richard and his co-founders, Jon Wright and Adam Bolon, raise that much-needed cash? Did they go to the bank? To venture capitalists? To the City? No. They sent an email to everyone they could think of that read "Do you know anybody very rich?"

Don't be fooled by the apparent ease with which Jon, Adam and Richard sent out that email. In essence, they had a network to die for. Not only did they know rich people, and people who knew rich people – but, equally importantly, those people took them seriously. They didn't label the email as spam and delete it. Instead, they read it and were prepared to act on it – which meant making time to assess the proposition, and to think about anybody else in their network who might be interested. Then they actually had to respond to it – by expressing interest and asking for more information and/or by forwarding it to other contacts, which means that they 'rated' the sender highly enough to put their own name on the line by allowing it to be used as a door opener. The whole process only works because the sender has networked actively, credibly and successfully in advance of needing that entrepreneurial capital.

There's lots of anecdotal evidence that networking is A Good Thing, but what about hard facts to show just how good it is – data that might shift your mindset away from passive acceptance of its benefits to active participation?

First out of the box is data concerning jobs from the UK's Office of National Statistics, whose surveys of the UK population ask people who have recently changed jobs two very pertinent questions. The first is "How did you get your current job?" Over 26% responded that it was through hearing from someone who worked there – networking, by any definition. But when the same group of people was asked a rather different question – "What is your main method of looking for work?", only 6.9% put asking friends, relatives and colleagues – networking – at the top of the list.[1]

1. Office for National Statistics, Annual Population Survey, July 2008–July 2009.

How Did You Get Your Current Job?

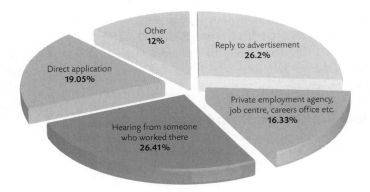

What Is Your Main Method Of Looking For Work?

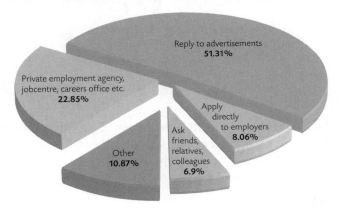

So there's an interesting, and quite dramatic mismatch here: just over 26% got jobs through networking but a mere 6.9% thought it was the most useful thing they could be doing to aid their job search.

IN A NUTSHELL

Most people underestimate the importance of networking when job-hunting. They probably underestimate its importance in almost every other sphere of their lives too...

This data covers the entire UK population, so you would be forgiven for asking whether the job-hunting picture is any different at senior levels? The answer is no: throughout the job search spectrum, networking is, to quote one piece of research, "a key factor in finding a new position"[2]. This same research, conducted among senior professionals around the world by Drake Beam Morin, an outplacement and career management firm, found the following figures:

How Professionals Find Work

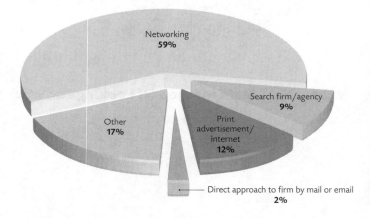

Networking
59%

Search firm/agency
9%

Other
17%

Print
advertisement/
internet
12%

Direct approach to firm by mail or email
2%

If we look at MBA graduates, the picture emphasises once again the crucial importance of networking. The sample size from a single business school is relatively small, so the data will fluctuate from year to year, but the overall pattern is crystal clear.

At London Business School, ranked first in the world by the *Financial Times*, the figures look like this:

- **In 2007, 25% of the full-time MBAs got their jobs by networking**

- **In 2008, the figure was 16%**

- **In 2009, 27% found post-MBA jobs through networking**

2. Drake Beam Morin, "Career Choices and Challenges of People in Transition Worldwide", 2006 (www.dbm.com).

Saïd Business School
UNIVERSITY OF OXFORD

At Saïd Business School in Oxford, the figures are very similar:

- **In 2007, 25% of their full-time MBAs got their jobs by networking**

- **In 2008, the figure was 26%**

Not convinced, or perhaps not relevant to your situation? Data on how interim managers (who typically take on short-term roles to lead change, relieve management pressures or tackle specific challenges) get their assignments show much the same pattern. For example, a study conducted in 2009, found that interims sourced an average of 65% of their projects through their own personal contacts, compared to 35% that came through agencies.[3]

CASE STUDY

From The Horse's Mouth

A straw poll, conducted for us by Eddie Mullen of Booster Interim Resources among members of an interim management group on LinkedIn, asked people what proportion of their assignments came via personal contacts and referrals.

Apart from the public sector (where the need to follow procedures alters the picture slightly), the overwhelming response was that networking is core to a successful interim career. Only 8 out of 65 respondents said they got more work from agencies than their personal contacts; another 6 said things were split pretty evenly 50:50. The remainder all said that their own network was crucial – with 17 people saying they sourced all their work themselves.

Here are a few quotes that we found interesting:

- **"In my experience, if you don't have a strong network and source of referrals, you'd better get a permanent job."**

continued overleaf

3. Executives Online, Interim Management Trend Update, 2009 (www.ExecutivesOnline.co.uk).

continued from previous page

- "In a tough market surely the key for all of us is to network like mad wherever and whenever and with whomever we can."

- "It is as important to have a good network of trusted contacts within the agents as it is to have good direct contacts."

- "In the two years since I left [my full-time job] only two paying jobs have come up that weren't directly from introductions or people that I know... The two that came from non-contact routes both happened because of people overhearing me advising a client on the phone, once on a train and the other in an airport lounge, and being interested enough in what they heard to introduce themselves."

The informal survey only asked about how people sourced their assignments. But anybody who has taken on an interim, or in fact any short-term, project will also know from experience that (a) an existing and supportive network is an essential resource in tackling the many challenges of such projects and (b) networking skills are vital if you are to hit the ground running and navigate your way through the maze of relationships and alliances that makes up any organisation.

Networking and onward referral is an important aspect of both sales and business development, but it amazes us how often people in these functions neglect to ask for a simple referral from a satisfied customer. Here's one company that has formalised the process and, although there is a small reward for making that referral, the key point is that no-one is going to put their own credibility on the line by doing so if they themselves haven't been happy with the service provided.

Recommend a friend.
You'll receive a gift and your friend will receive some great discounts.

that's the benefit of Benfield

More impressive than the data, however, and certainly more memorable, is this rather old but definitely gold ad from publisher McGraw Hill:

"*I don't know who you are.*
I don't know your company.
I don't know your company's product.
I don't know what your company stands for.
I don't know your company's customers.
I don't know your company's record.
I don't know your company's reputation.
Now—what was it you wanted to sell me?"

MORAL: Sales start **before** your salesman calls—with business publication advertising.

McGRAW-HILL MAGAZINES
BUSINESS•PROFESSIONAL•TECHNICAL

© The McGraw-Hill Companies, Inc. Reproduced with permission of The McGraw-Hill Companies, Inc.

What better reason to develop relationships and rapport than to avoid being in that particular firing line?

While on the subject of selling, we've already made the point that effective networking is about opening doors rather than closing sales, but sooner or later we all have to do some selling, whether it's widgets, an Olympic bid or ourselves. Writing in Harvard Business Review, academics Üstuner and Godes[4] make the point that each step of the sales 'funnel' requires the salesperson to bring into play a different subset of their network. While most will almost certainly do this

4. Tuba Üstuner and David Godes, "Better Sales Networks", *Harvard Business Review*, July-August, 2006).

intuitively, mapping out the different typologies used at each stage can serve as a useful template for success, as well as helping analyse and identify the potential gaps in your network.

To take just two segments of the sales process, let's look at initial prospecting and closing the deal. Any salesperson can make a list of obvious prospects with which to fill the mouth of the sales 'funnel'. But to get to the less obvious ones, or to get an introduction to the right person, involves activating a wide-ranging and diverse network of people who don't necessarily know each other but who do know lots of different people.

But when closing a complex deal, say Üstuner and Godes, a salesperson needs to be able to call on a trusted network of existing clients, willing to back up the salesperson's claims that the product or service on offer really does meet their needs. So what the salesperson now needs is a very different-looking network of referees, people to whom they have previously sold, and with whom they have stayed in touch.

IN A NUTSHELL

People buy people as much as they buy products or services. Networking is about building relationships of trust.

There's another very good reason for developing a networking culture if you are looking for business. Harvey Mackay wrote a book called *Dig Your Well Before You're Thirsty*. Credit where credit is due: it's a great title and the sentiment is bang on, as Chris Ingram experienced in the case study earlier in the chapter. But the sentiment is just as applicable in business development, in which effective networking can help with the problems caused by 'churning' and 'porpoising'.

Anyone in business development will tell you that the cost of acquiring a new customer is almost always much higher than keeping or growing an existing one. Yet how often do we (and companies) allow such wasteful churning to take place as we focus on meeting new people rather than developing existing relationships? 'Agency X wins client Y' may be a far sexier headline than 'Client Y still working with same old

Agency X', but the truth is that energy is best spent where it will be most productive.

'Porpoising' is the other business development bugbear, experienced in industries as diverse as public relations, clinical trials and luxury yacht building, which are typically plagued by a constant battle between feast and famine. If there's too little business, employees still have to be paid for doing nothing for as long as the company can bear the load (after which, disaster). If there's too much work, it's almost impossible to bring new people on board and 'up to speed' fast enough to do the new work as well as keeping existing clients satisfied. And if existing staff become overstretched and unhappy, the consequences for reputation and quality of work are obvious.

So where does networking fit into all of this? It impinges in two rather different ways. First, effective networking can bring early word not only of opportunities but also of potential future employees who can be brought on board quickly in the event of an upswing in business.

CASE STUDY

Round Pegs For Round Holes

When we asked for examples of how networking had improved the recruitment process at a global law firm, Eleni, a senior member of the business support team, had no difficulty providing two examples:

"On one occasion, I was speaking with a contact from HR in our German office about how useful it would be to have a foreign lawyer within our team, particularly a German one. She immediately put me in touch with someone she knew who had recently moved to London and who is now on our team!

"Similarly, I bumped into a partner in the street a few weeks ago and in the course of explaining how busy we were and desperate for technical legal help, she identified someone who is now a wonderful addition to our team on a short-term contract."

In both of Eleni's examples, she would have found the right person for the job eventually. But when you're busy, who wants to wade through dozens of unsuitable CVs? And in this era of tight budgets, networking saved on two hefty recruitment fees. Turning to her network for help brought multiple benefits – it saved Eleni trouble, it saved her employers money and it (presumably) gave her contacts a warm feeling, knowing that they had done a good turn for two friends: Eleni and the new hire.

The second reason why networking can help avoid porpoising relates to the old adage that "nothing succeeds like success". The time to be going out and generating new business is when you have a success story to shout about, not when you are trying to play 'catch up'. This plays to the bias of human psychology that one way in which we try to gain confidence that we have made the right decision is to copy the decisions of others.

DO TRY THIS

Dining Out

You're in Rome for a weekend's sightseeing and find yourself in the Piazza Navona at lunchtime. You see two pavement cafés next to each other with very similar menus and pretty much identical pricing. One restaurant is about half full with people obviously enjoying lunch and the other has one table occupied and waiters lounging around looking bored.

Which restaurant do you choose? Why?

Chances are you choose the busy restaurant, on the assumption that, if it is busy, it must be good. Not the strongest of evidence on which to base a decision, but nonetheless very powerful. But what if we now told you that restaurateurs have been known to offer free meals or even pay people to dine there simply to 'prime the pump' and create that all-important illusion of the busy eatery. It's the same principle used by buskers: putting a few coins of their own in the hat before playing a note removes a big mental hurdle for the potential donor by providing reassurance and reinforcement that if others have (apparently) contributed, then the music must be 'good' and worthy of support.

So, getting out there and networking with potential business contacts can encourage them to give you their business because your very success makes you either a scarce or a desirable commodity.

There's another reason to network most actively when the going is good as opposed to tough: our body language has a nasty habit of giving us away, and even your answer to as basic a question as "How's business?" can trigger all sorts of physiological responses that will set off conscious or unconscious alarm bells in the mind of your listener.

IN A NUTSHELL

Build your networks when things are good, before you need to draw on them for help.

And once you've landed your dream job, both the network you've built outside the organisation and the one you start to build internally will make a huge difference between success and failure, and will determine whether you become a trusted insider.

Nobody is likely to dispute the fact that we are naturally social animals and need ties to other people to function effectively. This is no less true at work than it is in our social lives. Imagine working in an organisation where people only talked about work, with no general or social chat; where the ties that linked you had no personal content. Would you feel that you belonged? That what you did mattered? Probably not. So, to feel included, to feel we belong, we need a network of people whom we like and respect. And if we don't feel we belong, we're likely to do a poor job and/or want to leave that organisation. So employee satisfaction, and career success are both linked to the building of strong, supportive networks.[5]

When faced with a problem or issue to resolve, we often need to turn to our network for help. If we don't know how to tackle something, with luck (and proactive networking) we will "know a man (or a woman) who can".

5. See, for example, Hans-Georg Wolf and Klaus Moser, "Effects of Networking on Career Success: A Longitudinal Study", *Journal of Applied Psychology*, Vol 94, No 1, 2009, pp. 196–206.

Your Eyes And Ears

Back in the 1960s, social psychologist Stanley Milgram undertook some seminal research into the 'small world phenomenon'.* In 2003, researchers at the Department of Sociology of Columbia University in New York decided to replicate that study, using up-to-date internet technology.

We'd heard about the research, but were hugely gratified to see our network swing into action as we received a flurry of emails from numerous sources telling us about it. Here's where some of the information came from:

■ Alan, who had attended a seminar-style presentation some months previously, told us about an article in the *Financial Times*

■ Brian, who had attended our workshop at Henley Management College, alerted us to a piece in the *Daily Mirror*

■ Rob, who had attended our workshop at Morgan Stanley six months earlier, referred us to another tabloid newspaper

■ Miles emailed us about the feature on the BBC website

■ And finally, Peter, a friend in New York, sent a link to the *New York Times*

All the articles referred to an article published in the journal *Science*. So Judith asked another friend, who is a librarian, to get her a copy of the original source article. Hey presto – a network in action!

* See Chapter 2, page 38 for more information.

Sometimes we find solutions within our inner circle, the relatively small number of people we know really well. But at other times, if the problem is more tricky or more unusual, we may have to look further afield. Our natural instinct is to cluster, to stick with the people whom we know best and trust the most. However, venturing further afield can bring huge rewards.

Ronald Burt, of the University of Chicago, has undertaken research that demonstrates this. He claims that innovation isn't necessarily born out of individual genius or, to use a well-worn cliché, 'blue-sky thinking'. Instead he argues that individuals who build diverse networks, so that they themselves become bridges between different social or professional groups, are at greater 'risk of having a good idea'. Why? Well, as he puts it: "An idea mundane in one group can be a valuable insight in another."[6]

Not rocket science, perhaps. But the idea that good, innovative ideas have 'social origins' is powerful nevertheless. In Burt's own succinct phrase, "This is not creativity born of genius; it is creativity as an import-export business."[7] Innovators aren't necessarily exceptionally smart people with exceptionally creative minds – bright sparks who think differently. They can be people just like you and me, who do two very important things differently: they mix with a wide variety of individuals, not just their close friends, and they listen as well as talk.

This is why many companies are realising that they need to encourage their staff to mingle both internally and with colleagues in the wider business network on a social, as well as a purely instrumental, level. Water coolers, canteens, social activities – all have a key role to play.

It's also why many corporations are turning to open innovation in order to maintain their competitive advantage. Instead of confining innovation within a fortress-like, internal 'R&D' lab, corporates such as P&G and GlaxoSmithKline are asking the network to provide new ideas and new solutions. Similarly, Karim Lakhani of Harvard Business School found that, often, it is "outsiders – those with expertise at the periphery of a problem's field – who were most likely to find answers and do so quickly".[8]

6. Ronald S Burt, "Structural Holes and Good Ideas", *American Journal of Sociology*, Vol 110 No 2, Sept 2004, pp. 349–399).

7. Ibid, page 388.

8. Karim Lakhani, "Open Source Science: A New Model for Innovation", *Working Knowledge*: Harvard Business School newsletter, November 20, 2006.

IN A NUTSHELL

Step outside your comfort zone. Just meeting people you already know and feel comfortable with doesn't extend your network or your reputation.

The benefits of socially generated innovation aren't confined to us as individuals, or even us 'joined together' as companies or organisations. Cities and societies can benefit from this too. Richard Florida of the University of Toronto has developed what he calls the 'gay concentration index'. The tolerance a city shows for gay people, it seems, correlates rather well with how successful that city is in today's fast-moving world. That's not because gay people are necessarily more creative or intelligent – but quite simply because diversity leads to innovation and innovation leads to prosperity. The gay concentration index is a shorthand technique for measuring diversity. To quote Richard Florida: "Cities with thriving arts and cultural climates and openness to diversity of all sorts...enjoy higher rates of innovation and high-wage economic growth."[9]

Returning to Burt for a moment, it's interesting to note that his analysis of the data he collected (about hundreds of managers running the supply chain in one of America's largest electronics companies, for example) revealed that these active networkers, these brokers between groups, reaped other benefits too: "more positive performance evaluations, faster promotions, higher compensation and more successful teams".[10] Put simply, by nurturing a wide-ranging network you are more likely to be successful in your career.

People who don't only mingle with colleagues in the same company, the same department or the same sector are more likely to be exposed to different ways of doing things. And so long as they are open enough to listen, creative enough to envisage possibilities, and perhaps humble enough to ask, they're able to transfer and adapt from one context to another, different one.

IN A NUTSHELL

Networking can't (and shouldn't) replace talent. But if you network actively, you have a far greater chance of having your talent recognised.

9. Richard Florida, *The Rise Of The Creative Class*, New York: Basic Books, 2003.

10. Burt, "Structural Holes", p. 354.

Leadership is a much-studied and often only partially understood phenomenon. From among the many strands that are part of the make up of an exceptional leader, we see at least one that stands out: acknowledging the importance of networking and being able to do it effectively. After detailed study of 30 emerging leaders, Herminia Ibarra and Mark Hunter, both from the top-ranking business school INSEAD, concluded that:

"What differentiates a leader from a manager, research tells us, is the ability to figure out where to go and to enlist the people and groups necessary to get there. Recruiting stakeholders, lining up allies and sympathizers, diagnosing the political landscape, and brokering conversations among unconnected parties are all part of a leader's job... Aspiring leaders must learn to build and use strategic networks... They must accept that networking is one of the most important requirements of their new leadership roles."[11]

Enough said?

Before we end this chapter, let's not leave our personal lives out of the picture. In times of distress, our network is our back-up, our safety net. Take this story of how the network can spring into action when there's a crisis.

CASE STUDY

A Friend In Need

Stuart is passionate about networking, and works with a major HR consultancy to help people manage career transitions. As Stuart himself says: "My wife and I have had a number of setbacks in our lives, the most painful having been the accidental death of our 19-year-old daughter Laura in a freak car accident.

"One of the things that enabled Gael (my wife) and I to survive this nightmare was the 'army' of instant proactive support that just emerged out of nowhere to help take care of us. You just don't realise how powerful a network can be until you really need the support."

11. Herminia Ibarra and Mark Hunter, "How Leaders Create and Use Networks", *Harvard Business Review*, January 2007, pp. 40-47.

It's when the chips are down that you realise how much you need your network of friends, contacts and acquaintances for practical (and emotional) help.

This is an extreme situation, of course, and we hope that none of you ever have to put your network to the test in this way. To balance the scales, here's a much less dramatic example. (And we're sure that, if you reflect for a moment, you'll be able to come up with numerous examples of how your own network has supported you as you go about your daily life.)

CASE STUDY

Let The Train Take The Strain

Kishore, who attended a workshop in 2007, told us this story:

"I was travelling to London, and got chatting to a lady on the train. In true English fashion, our conversation started with the weather! But she quickly guessed that I was from India, and began to tell me about her trip there. I soon learnt that she was a teacher, and provided private tuition for kids.

"It so happened that I was looking for a tutor to help my son with his exams, and wasn't sure where to look. We exchanged contact details, and she helped me find a tutor. She has since also helped my wife develop her teaching career.

"And all that came from a 20 minute conversation on a train!"

IN A NUTSHELL

Networking is as much about giving as about receiving help.

It shouldn't be forgotten that access to a network empowers not only the individual but also the group. After all, what are political parties, trade unions or nations if not networks? Special interest groups, be they women's, ethnic or just your local public library user group, can be transformational.

We hope this chapter has convinced you that networking isn't an optional extra. It is, without a doubt, a 'must have' in all these areas:

So get out there, and get networking. Read on for some ideas on how to do it, and do it well. In case you need any more words of encouragement, here's another quote from INSEAD professor Herminia Ibarra:

"We have seen over and over again that people who work at networking can learn not only how to do it well but also how to enjoy it. And they tend to be more successful in their careers..."[12]

12. Ibid, p.47.

CHAPTER TWO

It's a Small World... So What?

"Mr. Bond, they have a saying in Chicago: 'Once is happenstance, twice is coincidence, the third time it's enemy action.'"

IAN FLEMING *Goldfinger*

It really is a very small world, and most of us have had the experience of meeting someone for the first time and being astonished by the 'coincidence' that we have acquaintances or even friends in common... it even happens at our workshops.

Cards On The Table

Alistair and Ajay sat next to each other all day at one of our workshops. They'd never met before and worked in very different industries. But they chatted at breaks and paired up for one of the role plays.

When Ajay got home that evening he spread out the business cards he'd collected from his fifteen or so fellow attendees on the kitchen table. His brother Rajay, who happened to be visiting that evening, immediately spotted Alistair's card and exclaimed "Hey, I know him... how do you come to have his business card?" It just so happens that Rajay is an ex-colleague of Alistair's but had lost touch with him. It also just happens that Rajay had recently been made redundant and was looking for a job.

Rajay emailed Alistair the very next day and they arranged to meet. The outcome? Alistair introduced Rajay to an employer who was recruiting, and Rajay has introduced Alistair to some potential clients.

Why do such apparent coincidences occur? Part of the explanation lies in the fact that one of the first things a skilled networker does when meeting a stranger is to try to establish some common ground on which to base a conversation.

But a more important part of the explanation for this phenomenon lies in what has become known as the 'small-world problem'; though quite why it's a 'problem' we've never understood. Back in 1967, the social psychologist Stanley Milgram was intrigued by the question of the connectivity of human society. Were communities well connected with each other, or did society function as a series of discrete and not very well linked units?

To test this, Milgram conducted a series of experiments.[1] In one, he wrote to a random selection of 160 residents of Omaha, Nebraska, asking for help with "a study of social contact in American society". To those who responded, Milgram sent a document containing the name of a stockbroker in Boston, Massachusetts and the instruction that "if you do not know the target person on a personal basis, do not try to contact him directly. Instead, mail this folder...to a personal acquaintance who is more likely than you to know the target person...it must be someone you know on a first-name basis."

As you can see from the map, Nebraska is hardly next door to Boston, so when Milgram asked an "intelligent friend" how many steps they thought it might take to successfully negotiate the country's geographic and social hurdles, the answer came back that "he estimated it would take 100 intermediate persons or more" to cover such a huge distance.

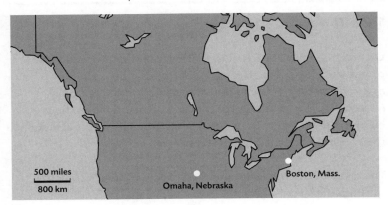

What actually happened has become part of sociology folklore. Although many of the 160 packages didn't get through to the stockbroker, of those that did reach their final destination, the majority had got there in only five or six steps (some arriving in as few as two and some with as many as ten – but no higher than that).

As an aside, the fact that not all the packages reached the stockbroker is interesting in itself. Despite the experimenter's impeccable academic credentials and the fact that postage costs were covered, some people just couldn't be bothered to make the minimal effort asked of them.

1. Stanley Milgram, "The Small-World Problem", *Psychology Today*, Vol 1, No 1, May 1967, pp. 61–67.

This highlights the difference between a database and a network. Just knowing somebody (even worse, knowing of somebody) simply isn't enough. For a network to really work, so to speak, the people in it have to have a relationship with each other. They don't need to be best friends, but there does have to be at least some warmth.

Milgram's finding has become embodied in the notion that we are only (on average) six steps away from anyone else on the planet. The phrase 'six degrees of separation' has become almost commonplace, and many of us take this connectedness for granted – but at the time that the research was carried out, this was ground-breaking stuff. Remember, Milgram's colleague guessed that it would take 80–100 steps, so to find that it happened in as few as six was something of a revelation. But why so few connections? The answer is in the maths, and it can be illustrated using one of the most pivotal events in recent history.

CASE STUDY

Twin Towers

On 11 September 2001, H. Russell Bernard from the Department of Anthropology at the University of Florida, got a call from a reporter asking: "Are you the same person who studied the Mexico City earthquake?" The reporter wanted to know how many people in the US would be affected directly by the attack on the World Trade Center and the Pentagon.

The result of this conversation was a paper entitled "Estimating the Ripple Effect of a Disaster", which appeared in *Connections*, the journal of the International Network for Social Network Analysis. According to this paper, less than one American in 200 was likely to have actually known one of those who died in the tragedy ('known' being defined for these purposes as "A knows B by sight or name; A can contact B in person by telephone or by mail; and A has had contact with B in the past two years").

However, with each American knowing (under the definition above) a minimum of 290 people – a figure that has held up well as an average across five studies, despite the fact that the number would be larger if everyone had their address books to hand at the time of survey – the estimate was that about 83% of the US population were only two steps removed from one of the 6,333 missing in the attacks at the time the paper was written.[2]

So how do we get from 'almost nobody' (fewer than one in 200) who knows someone who died to 'almost everybody' (83% of the population) in a single step? Let's use some simple maths rather than the complex statistical method employed in the 'Ripple' paper.

Suppose for a moment that we live in a rather sad world where everyone only knows two people but none of those people know each other (not a very highly networked community!). What that means is that, if you asked a friend to introduce you to their friends, there would be two new people to whom they could direct you. If you then went to each of them and asked to be introduced to their friends, each of those friends could add another two new faces to your network and theirs. Repeat the same process, and you get what's illustrated in the diagram below:

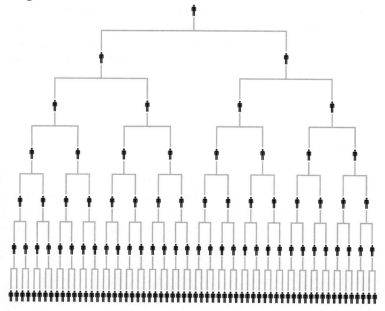

2. H. Russell Bernard et al, "Estimating the Ripple Effect of a Disaster", *Connections*, Vol. 24, No. 2, 2001, pp. 30–34, published by ISNA (International Network for Social Network Analysis).

Within six steps – the 'six degrees of separation' that Milgram described – we've gone from knowing only 2 people to knowing 64.

The Power Of Doubling

Imagine you're about to play a round of golf, and your partner suggests doubling the stakes at each hole, starting at just £1 for the first hole. Would you accept? Any idea what the stakes would be at the 18th hole? If not, we suggest that you quickly do the sums, which will make you realise you should only accept the offer if you're absolutely confident of beating your opponent, or have very deep pockets. (The answer is at the foot of the page.)

In reality, of course, we don't live in this fictionally isolated world and, far from knowing just two acquaintances, most of us have a network of at least hundreds (and often thousands) of friends, relatives, colleagues and acquaintances. So, instead of just doubling at each extra stage of separation, the numbers rack up at an even more astounding rate.

Let's be highly conservative and say that everyone has 100 acquaintances. At the first step of separation, you theoretically have access not only to your 100 acquaintances but to the 100 acquaintances of your acquaintances: 10,000 people. At the third step, that multiplies by 100 again to become 1,000,000. At the fourth step it becomes 100,000,000. At the fifth step 10 billion, so that we run out of people on the planet even before we reach the sixth step.

So something appears to be wrong with the maths if we're arriving at such astounding numbers.

Actually, there's nothing wrong with the numbers themselves, it's just that we haven't yet factored in one crucial point, and it's the same point that ensures that chain letters and pyramid selling schemes rarely work for very long (if at all) – and that's the fact that if you know 1,000 people and your friend knows 1,000 people, the chances are that there will be some degree of overlap between who you know and who your friend knows. The wider you cast the net, the greater the overlap.

Answer
Starting with a £1 stake, and doubling the stakes at each hole, the stake at the 18th would be a whopping £131,072.

Since we're not interested in meeting everybody on the planet, however, this overlap and the resulting reduction in the numbers doesn't invalidate our point. The simple truth is that we can all reach far more people than we realised on first thought. And we rarely need to go through six steps to get where we want to go: the path is often much, much shorter than we anticipate. That, of course, is a good thing – because, in reality, a chain of links that has to pass through six handshakes is almost certain to break.

IN A NUTSHELL

The world is a smaller place than we realise.

So, if we're all better connected than we realise, is networking simply a numbers game? The answer is both yes and no, but let's start with the 'yes'. Consider the following questions:

■ **Who do you know who might be interested in funding your great new business idea?**

■ **Who do you know who might help with the job hunt?**

■ **Who do you know who could give advice on employment law?**

■ **Who do you know who could describe what it's like to live and work in Aberdeen?**

These typical questions all have something in common. They involve fishing in a pretty small pond of people you know directly. It may be, of course, that you're personally extremely well connected and always know the right person to talk to. But most of us aren't that well connected: if we stay within our 'comfort zone' of familiarity, the chances are we won't get the help we need. To find the right people to help us, we have to go fishing in the much bigger pond of the people we don't know directly but who know the people we know.

There's no better way to explain why that is so than to quote an article by Malcolm Gladwell in *The New Yorker* magazine entitled "Six Degrees of Lois Weinberg":

The sociologist Mark Granovetter interviewed several hundred professional and technical workers from the Boston suburb of Newton, asking them in detail about their employment history. He found that almost fifty-six per cent of those he talked to had found their jobs through a personal connection, about twenty per cent had used formal means (advertisements, head-hunters), and another twenty per cent had applied directly. This much is not surprising: the best way to get in the door is through a personal contact. But the majority of those personal connections, Granovetter found, did not involve close friends. They were what he called "weak ties." Of those who used a contact to find a job, for example, only 16.7 per cent saw that contact "often," as they would have if the contact had been a good friend; 55.6 per cent saw their contact only "occasionally"; and 27.8 per cent saw the contact "rarely." People were getting their jobs not through their friends but through acquaintances.

Granovetter argued that when it comes to finding out about new jobs – or, for that matter, gaining new information, or looking for new ideas – weak ties tend to be more important than strong ties. Your friends, after all, occupy the same world that you do. They work with you, or live near you, and go to the same churches, schools, or parties. How much, then, do they know that you don't know? Mere acquaintances, on the other hand, are much more likely to know something that you don't. To capture this apparent paradox, Granovetter coined a marvellous phrase: "the strength of weak ties." The most important people in your life are, in certain critical realms, the people who aren't closest to you, and the more people you know who aren't close to you the stronger your position becomes.[3]

To quote Granovetter directly:

In many cases, the contact [through whom a respondent got their job] was someone only *marginally* included in the current field of contacts, such as an old college friend or a former workmate or employer, with whom

3. Malcolm Gladwell, "Six Degrees of Lois Weinberg", The New Yorker, 11 January 1999.

sporadic contact had been maintained.... It is remarkable that people receive *crucial information from individuals whose very existence they have forgotten*.

The bold italics in the quotation are ours, to highlight the counter-intuitive fact that real, useful and important information often comes not from our close circle of friends but from people on the periphery of our networks.

Knowing lots of people can be as important as knowing just a few people really well.

Turning that on its head you can see that, in order to put ourselves in the stream of this information flow, we have to go out there and build those 'weak tie' networks.

CASE STUDY

The Clever Way To Find A Job

Nicola, a learning and development specialist, told us:

"Some years ago, I was working for a firm of chartered accountants and wasn't particularly happy in my job. One morning, I bumped into a 'dinner party acquaintance' commuting into work. She worked for a large oil company and asked me if I was enjoying my current job, as her boss was looking for someone for a particular role there. I told her that I certainly was interested in making a change, and she duly emailed the job spec to me. Within a week, I had met her boss and signed a contract!"

We chose this case study, from among the many that we have heard, because it exemplifies the power of weak ties. With minimal effort on her part, Nicola secured a good job with a blue chip company – and hasn't looked back since. She herself told us that, if she hadn't met her acquaintance, the chances of her hearing about the vacancy would have been close to zero.

Don't Follow Your Instincts

Next time you go to a party, a conference or a reunion, make a point of not heading straight for people you already know. It may be a natural, and perfectly understandable, instinct – but in some cases, those instincts simply lead you in the wrong direction. Instead, make a point of meeting new people, of creating new (weak) ties – they may be the very ones that, at some point in the future, help you to take a vital step that may change your life.

Nicola's good fortune came about through serendipity, through a chance conversation. But, looked at another way, all this means that (at least in theory) you should be able to deliberately connect with the Queen, the Prime Minister, the President or the rock star of your choice. Clearly, it's not quite that easy, so what are the magic ingredients that can help turn theory into practice?

We've told you it's a small world, but don't take our word for it. For you to be fired up enough to try to make connections that you'd never have had the patience, lateral thought or belief in yourself to make in the past, we think we need to demonstrate to you that the world really is small.

The Internet Movie Database (IMDB) is an online database that, among other things, includes every actor and actress who has ever been in a Hollywood movie. At the time of writing, the IMDB contained the names of over a million actors, although the exact number changes as new movies are made and new actors make their debuts. So this is a living database, which contains pretty much all the members of the movie acting profession, and as such it makes a rather interesting research tool.

Enter Brett Tjaden from the University of Virginia's computer science department, who in 1996 decided it would be interesting to build on the existing concept of 'Erdös numbers' (how people linked to the mathematician Paul Erdös) and chart the relationships between actors in the IMDB.

Choosing the actor Kevin Bacon as the starting point (because, according to Wikipedia, the game's inventors watched two Kevin Bacon movies during a snowstorm and got to thinking about his connections), Tjaden created what has become known as the Oracle of Bacon to chart how actors in the IMDB relate to Kevin Bacon. Here's how it works: if you have been in a movie with Kevin Bacon, you have a 'Bacon number' of 1 (that is, one degree of separation). If you have been in a movie with someone who has been in a movie with Kevin Bacon, then you have a Bacon number of 2 (two degrees of separation), and so on.

You'd think that with a database of over a million names, it wouldn't be too difficult to find actors who are a long way removed from Bacon. Why not try it yourself and see?

DO TRY THIS

Bringing Home The Bacon

Home of the Oracle of Bacon is www.oracleofbacon.org. Don't read on at this stage; just dive in with the names of a few actors and see what Bacon numbers they return.

Surprised by the result? You've probably chosen some well-known names that would naturally be 'top of mind' so, before you go further, choose an actor who represents each one of the following:

- **An actor from the days of the 'golden silents'**

- **An actor from a non-English-speaking country**

- **The Shakespearian actor of your choice.**

Surprised by what you found this time? Did you manage to find anybody with a Bacon number of 4? Did you get stuck at 3 or 2? It really is much more difficult than intuition would suggest to find people who are not connected quite closely to Kevin Bacon.

But why our suggestion about choosing actors from specific genres? It's to make the important point not only that networks can cut across time (silent films to the present), geography (international films and actors) and industry sectors (Shakespeare to tinsel town) but that a connection that appears to be a complete long shot can paradoxically become an excellent shortcut.

As you'll see from the table below, it really is rather difficult to find people in the IMDB who are more than four steps away from Kevin.

Bacon Number	Number of People
0	1
1	2,356
2	225,092
3	673,852
4	155,598
5	9,894
6	846
7	143
8	15

Total number of linkable actors: **1,067,797**
Weighted total of linkable actors: **3,152,155**
Average Kevin Bacon number: **2.952**

So the next time you find yourself thinking "I don't know anyone who can introduce me to X" or "I've got no way of getting an introduction to company Y", remember the Oracle and the tools we're about to offer. And for anyone who thinks that they can hide behind the defence that the Oracle doesn't reflect real life, let us remind you that the Oracle of Bacon is a real database of real people in a real industry.

But the Oracle hasn't finished with us yet. Having established the Bacon number of everyone in the IMDB, it's possible with enough time and computing power to rank every actor in the database in terms of their degree of connectedness. The picture that emerges is interesting in its own right, but it also offers another insight that has ramifications for practical networking.

Any thoughts before we reveal all as to the most connected movie actor? At the time of writing (and this can change because the IMDB is constantly updated), the most connected actor was Dennis Hopper, with a 'Hopper Number' of 2.743 across his 199 screen credits (see http://oracleofbacon.org/center_list.php for the top 1000 names at the "Center of the Hollywood Universe").

But how is it that Udo Kier (whose name was unknown to either of us before we started researching this book) comes out at number four in terms of connectivity, while a household name such as Arnold Schwarzenegger languishes in 314th position (which in relative terms is still pretty healthy, given that there are well over a million actors in the database)?

Ask yourself what sort of movies Udo Kier makes and you might be hard pushed to define any given genre – although apparently he likes making horror films. You might even be forgiven for not being able to name any specific movie. Ask the same question about Schwarzenegger and images of a muscle-bound torso and action movies are likely to come to mind.

Leaving aside his political activities and connections, Schwarzenegger's movie life could be compared with an anthill – repeatedly doing the same sorts of thing with the same sorts of people. Kier's world is more like a Noah's Ark, working with different people on different projects, and so amassing not just more but also *different* types of connections as his career progresses.

Of course, you could turn that argument on its head and ask how Christopher Lee, best known to us as Dracula, manages to secure a place in the top 15. The answer is that, despite the typecasting and the prolific work on low budget Hammer films with small casts, Lee has also appeared in high budget films with large casts, such as *The Lord of the Rings*. The sheer variety of people with whom Lee has worked over a long career makes him exceptionally well connected.

So what is the relevance of all this movie talk to the business of effective, real-life networking?

What the Oracle shows so graphically is that the overall effectiveness of an individual's network is a function not only of quantity (in the Oracle's case, how many movies) but also of quality (different types of movie, genre and length of active career). The clear lesson for us lesser mortals from consulting the Oracle is that we should think about not just how many people we know but the *variety* of people we know.

We've already shown from Granovetter's work on weak ties that the more people you know, the more likely you are to receive (and, of course, be able to offer) interesting and useful new information. And that's about as far as many networkers seem to get. But those counter-intuitive 'weak ties' of Granovetter are so productive not just because of the number of contacts but also because of their variety. To repeat our previous analogy, if you live and work in an 'anthill' in which most of the people around you have the same sort of age, background, skill set and experience, then the chances are that everyone around you will have access to very similar information, and will have similar mindsets and ideas about jobs or business opportunities. It's those people who live and work in rather different environments from yours who are often likely to offer the best route to new information and insights.

Nathalie Learns How Not To Network

Nathalie, an experienced and confident networker whose professional life centres on alumni relations, told us this story from early in her career:

"It was my first ever professional conference and I was feeling a little daunted being there alone with over five hundred other delegates. However, I was reassured by the fact that our badges all had stickers on them, with different colours for different branches of our profession.

"Walking around the exhibitors' hall during a break on the first day, I saw someone walking towards me and decided it was time I started to develop my networking skills. So I smiled at the approaching gentleman and looked hopeful. His response rather surprised me. He looked at my badge, saw the yellow sticker on it and said, 'Oh, you work in alumni relations, no, that's no use!' and with that he changed direction and walked away, leaving me standing, open-mouthed, and wondering why a communications professional thought he had nothing to say to, or nothing in common with, someone in alumni relations!"

Nathalie might not have been working in exactly the same area as the gentleman in question, but he was clearly so mentally short-sighted that he was cutting himself off from any useful intelligence that she might have been able to offer. We see more subtle examples of the same attitude played out over and over again: for example, members of an orchestra not wanting to talk to bankers because they have "nothing in common". Excuse us, but just take a look at arts sponsorship! And how does the banker who specialises in looking after High Net Worth individuals know that the husband, wife, father, sister, brother or great aunt of a threadbare-looking and underpaid second violin isn't as rich as Croesus and looking for a safe home for their spare cash?

Or take the following story, again provided by Nathalie.

CASE STUDY

Birds Of A Feather

"Every year groups of students from my business school would travel to different parts of the world to explore the way business was conducted in that country or region. Along with formal meetings and lunches, we also provided the opportunity to meet with alumni at informal drinks receptions. After one particular visit to Hong Kong I was surprised by some of the student feedback I elicited. When I asked if the event had been a success, one student responded: 'Well no, not really. You see, I want to work in investment banking and all the people at the event were management consultants so they were no use to me at all.'

continued overleaf

continued from previous page

"I was rather bewildered by this and asked if he had tried to explore whether these management consultants had any useful connections to whom they might be able to introduce him. 'I don't know!' was his response. 'When I found out they were management consultants and therefore of no use to me I just went off and got drunk with my friends.'"

As Nathalie said, "I doubt if that particular student will go far, unless he finds a way of shedding his blinkers and seeing the world as it really is. Don't management consultants and investment bankers ever talk to each other? Don't, in fact, investment bankers often employ management consultants?"

DO TRY THIS

Expand Your Network

Next time you find yourself in any social or professional gathering of people, make a point of talking to at least one new person. Most of us naturally gravitate towards people whom we already know, avoiding the challenge of making new connections. But, in truth, this is wasting a golden opportunity to establish links to people who inhabit a world that is slightly different from your own – to create a new 'weak tie', in fact.

We'll leave further anecdotes about the benefits of networking till later in this book. Since this chapter is primarily dedicated to outlining the ideas that should underpin the techniques we're going to introduce (i.e. the strategy that supports the tactics), we'd like to introduce you to the concept of the 'small-world network'.

Up to this point, we've been happy to work with the 'six degrees of separation' view of the world as a means of encouraging you to believe that it really is much easier to find and harness connections than you might intuitively have thought. But there's another piece of this jigsaw that we now need to slot into place, in the shape of an article in the form of a letter from two scientists named Duncan J. Watts and Steven

H. Strogatz. Entitled "Collective Dynamics of 'Small-World' Networks", the letter appeared in the June 1998 issue of the respected science journal *Nature*.[5]

Almost everyone will have seen footage of fish swimming in a shoal, moving and turning almost as a single organism. While we know that fish possess a set of nerves along their bodies called the lateral line that helps them to sense and respond to the proximity and movement of their neighbours, this doesn't explain how two distant edges of a shoal can move in unison. If each fish were only sensing the position of its immediate neighbours, the movement of a shoal would look more like the ripple of a Mexican wave in a football stadium, as each fish moves slightly later than the one next to it.

But that's not what happens, and it turns out that the reason why not is explained by what Watts and Strogatz dubbed the 'small-world network'. It is not the function of this book to go into the maths of these phenomena (and a very good account has already been given by Mark Buchanan in his book *Small World*[6]), but the essential element is that, while most fish in the shoal are sensing only the movement of their close neighbours, a small number of fish take their cue instead from others much further away, so keeping the whole show in sync. If we accept that the instruction "swim up, swim down, swim left, swim right" is actually data being transmitted through a network, what we're seeing is most data being transmitted locally rather slowly but some data being transmitted over long distances extremely quickly for onward local transmission.

What those who model these networks mathematically have done is to work out just how many of these long-distance 'connectors' are necessary to create the fast transmission of data and multiple redundancy (if one or more fish gets eaten, the shoal can still move as one without breaking down) that is characteristic of these small-world networks. The answer is far fewer than anyone expected, which is one reason why these networks are so intriguing: throw a surprisingly small number of long-distance connections into an otherwise local network and the operation of that network changes dramatically.

The relevance of all this to our practical networking activity is that it turns out that human social networks are also small-world networks. The reality is that we're not all connected to each other by six degrees

5. D. J. Watts and S. H. Strogatz, "Collective Dynamics of 'Small-World' Networks", *Nature*, No 393 (6684), 1998, pp. 440–442.

6. Mark Buchanan, *Small World: Uncovering Nature's Hidden Networks*, London: Phoenix, 2002, p. 259.

of separation: we're actually all connected to each other through a surprisingly small number of very highly connected individuals.

This fact was borne out by the results of Stanley Milgram's 'chain letter' experiment that we described at the beginning of this chapter. Of the 64 packets that reached the stockbroker,

- **16 were delivered to his home by a Mr Jacobs.**

- **10 reached him at his work via a Mr Jones.**

- **5 were sent to him at his work by a Mr Brown.**

This means that almost 48% of all the packets were delivered by just three people – people who acted as funnels, channelling contact with our stockbroker. Viewed another way, these three people represent the difference between the metaphor of a network as smooth porridge (everyone connected to each other in a relatively homogenous matrix) versus lumpy porridge, in which a few densely connected lumps sit in a rather less densely populated sea.

The truth of this model was demonstrated very neatly by Malcolm Gladwell in his book *The Tipping Point*[7], in which he described an elegant, if rough and ready, experiment for demonstrating that some people are much better connected than others. Gladwell chose 250 names at random from the Manhattan telephone directory and asked people to score how many acquaintances they had with surnames the same as those on the page. Repeating the same experiment with different groups, including, for example, students, academics and professionals, Gladwell's results (which we've conflated for simplicity) looked something like this.

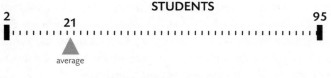

7. Malcolm Gladwell, *The Tipping Point: How Little Things Can Make a Big Difference*, London: Abacus, 2000, p. 279.

What does this tell us? In the first place, the average for students (at 20.96, to be precise) was about half that for the professionals (at 39) – which isn't too surprising, since the size of your network is obviously likely to be affected by how long you've been around to meet people. More interesting, though, is the fact that, at least in terms of number of acquaintances, some people are very well connected whereas others are quite isolated. Some people only knew as few as 2 or 16 people; at the other extreme were the really well-connected people who listed around 100 names. As we'll see shortly, becoming networked into those 'lumps in the porridge', or becoming a 'lump' yourself, is one element in creating a far-reaching and effective network.

However, when we talk about finding 'lumps' – or connectors as they're officially called – we're most definitely not talking about doing so from a manipulative viewpoint: it's simply that there are some people out there whose personality is such that they are naturally very good at getting to know people and collecting (and remembering) names, and enjoy introducing people to each other just to be helpful and to 'see what happens'. Here are some revealing thoughts from one very well-known and influential connector, Carole Stone:

> **I've always had an irresistible urge to make sure 'this person' meets 'that person'... Wherever there are two or three, or lots of people, gathered together, I want to be there... The excitement I get is in thinking that something big could come of a meeting between people I've put together.** [8]

And here's a nice example of how the involvement of a 'connector' can make a huge difference to the direction of a campaign.

CASE STUDY

Little Black Book

In 2009, the science writer Simon Singh was sued for libel by the British Chiropractic Association for questioning chiropractors' claims about the efficacy of their methods.

continued overleaf

8. Carole Stone, "Steve's Just Dying to Meet You", *New Statesman*, 10 April 2000.

continued from previous page

According to *The Independent* newspaper, a host of celebrities supported Singh's case – including the scientist Richard Dawkins, the comedian Harry Hill, the actors Ricky Gervais and Stephen Fry, and the author Martin Amis. Although it's easy to see why they should all have an interest in changing the UK's libel laws, how did they all come to rally behind this particular cause?

The answer, it seems, lies in the network of Peter Florence, actor and founder of the Hay Festival of Literature. Making good use of his extensive network, Florence emailed everybody who has spoken at the festival, asking for their support.

We particularly like this case study because it provides proof that active and intelligent networking can bring benefits to individuals, organisations *and* society at large.

Connectors don't wear badges saying "Talk to me, I'm a connector", so you'll have to rely on your instincts to identify them. Most of us, though, can think of someone at work or in our private lives who always seems to be in the thick of things, who knows who's who and what's what – and who is generous with their contacts. Someone who thrives in several different worlds simultaneously and is able to 'bridge the gap' between countries, industries, professions, social groups – the list is endless. Just think back to the Oracle of Bacon, and the actor-connectors who bridge the gap between different movie genres.

If you've done an MBA, or are professionally involved in learning and development or HR, you may have come across Meredith Belbin's work on building effective teams. His premise, in a nutshell, is that an effective team needs diversity and complementarity – different people fulfilling different roles. One of those, termed the 'Resource Investigator', sounds to us uncannily like a connector. Here's a description of the role:

> **Resource Investigators are often enthusiastic, quick-off-the-mark extroverts. They are good at communicating with people both inside and outside the company. They are natural negotiators and are adept at exploring new opportunities and developing contacts... As the name**

suggests, they are skilled at finding out what is available and what can be done. They usually receive a warm reception from others because of their own outgoing nature... Resource Investigators have relaxed personalities with a strong inquisitive sense and a readiness to see the possibilities in anything new.[9]

IN A NUTSHELL

Look out for connectors and recognise the value they bring.

In later chapters, we'll pick apart and analyse the skills such people possess, because it is quite possible to model and acquire at least some of those attributes. As Belbin's work shows (and as we all know), we are all different. Not everyone can, or should try to, become a classic connector; but all of us, without exception, should allow the concept to influence the way we behave. We should make a conscious effort to put people together, to foster relationships between people in our own network who may have plenty in common but don't know each other.

The reason we've focussed on personality as the main characteristic of a connector is that some people have very large networks by dint of the job they do or their environment, but either make a conscious choice not to share their contacts (falsely believing that this will diminish their personal power) or else simply fail to recognise the opportunities that exist for – and the benefits that accrue from – making referrals and acting as that vital short cut that keeps small-world networks going.

If you're in the former camp, we'd like to show you that being prepared to use your network for the benefit of others can ultimately benefit rather than erode your own personal power and reputation. If you're in the latter camp, we want you to take away the message that, by thinking actively about how you can harness your network rather than treating it as a passive by-product of your working and social life, you can create real long-term benefit for yourself.

As the point of this chapter is to tie the practical techniques that we're going to suggest to a sound strategic basis, don't take our word for what we've just said, try it yourself.

9. R. Meredith Belbin, *Management Teams: Why They Succeed or Fail*, London: Heinemann, 1981 (quotation reproduced by kind permission of Belbin Associates).

Demonstrate by your actions that you are a connector and people will flock to be connected to you. The rich really do get richer!

A simple thought experiment demonstrates the essential truth of this proposition. Let's imagine first that a colleague or friend asks you for help making a connection in company X. Let's further imagine that you are someone who is either reluctant to share your connections, doesn't have many connections to share or perhaps just doesn't stop to think about who's in your address book. So your response to the enquiry is that you can't help. Repeat that process a few times and your reputation becomes one of the truncated chain – not worth asking, because the answer will always be 'no' and people get fed up of being turned down over and over again to the point where they stop asking, or even communicating.

Imagine instead that you're someone who is prepared not only to share your connections but also to take the time and trouble to think creatively about how to help your friends and colleagues make the connections they need. In this scenario, you become known as someone who is generous with information, which encourages people to approach you and, crucially, to point others in your direction. You become a long chain and a magnet for further connections.

DO TRY THIS

Matchmaker, Matchmaker

1. Jot down the name of someone you've met in the past month. It may have been an informal chat, at a business meeting or during a conference or networking event.

2. Now jot down some 'stream of consciousness' bullet points about who they are, what interests and motivates them, and possibly their ambitions and aspirations.

3. With those bullet points to guide you, think about all the other people you know, and try to do some matchmaking. Who do you know who is involved in the same industry, or has similar interests? In other words, who could you introduce them to, just to see what happens.

4. Just do it! Write the email introducing 'Christopher to Michael' or 'Julie to James' with an indication as to why it might be useful for them to connect – then sit back and see what (if anything) happens.

While nothing astonishing may come about as a result of this first attempt to bring people together, the aim of the game is to cultivate a connecting frame of mind so that you see the links more easily in the future.

If you're hesitating, please be reassured that we aren't suggesting that you spend your entire time introducing people to each other – we would recommend doing it only when you think there genuinely is common ground. And, of course, you need to ensure that you don't give valuable referrals to people who will abuse your good nature (and vice versa, of course). We'll deal with the issue of giving and getting connections in the next chapter.

CHAPTER THREE

Hunting and Gathering, Giving and Getting

I find that the harder I work,
the more luck I seem to have.

THOMAS JEFFERSON *(US President, 1801–1809)*

As with so much in business, and indeed life in general, making good decisions comes down to having good information. Getting that information is actually a product of two factors that are often conflated in people's minds and need disentangling if we're to function optimally. These are:

1. Identifying a good source of information

2. Effectively harnessing that information source.

There's a certain breed of person who tells you about the 'quality' of their address book within minutes of meeting them. But knowing the CEOs of Alpha Corp, Bravo Industries or Charlie plc or having an address book full of celebrities may not actually be very useful if those people can't or won't help you get where you want to go – or if you can't (or don't) do anything for them.

Of course, there may be times when being on first name terms with the CEOs of the leading companies is incredibly useful, but too concentrated a focus on the top person can signal a failure to recognise that the most helpful and influential people are not necessarily at the top of the tree or in the public eye. Consider what happened to us on a business trip to Warsaw.

CASE STUDY

Tell Them Ewa Sent You

We were developing a business in Poland, and needed help finding our way around an unfamiliar market. Quite early on, a contact suggested we get in touch with the British Polish Chamber of Commerce, so we duly made an appointment to see Ewa, PA to the CEO of the Warsaw office.

To our shame, we can still remember thinking, as we rode the lift, that the meeting was bound to be a waste of time. After all, what help could a mere secretary provide? With the 20:20 vision that comes with hindsight, we realise now how wrong we were then.

Ewa listened attentively as we outlined our project. And when we told her that we needed to find, say, flexible office space, or a reliable translator, or a fulfilment house, her response was "Try so-and-so" or "I think so-and-so might be able to help with that".

And every time we called people and mentioned Ewa's name, we were given a hearing. Clearly it was up to us to sound credible... but in each case, it was Ewa's name that opened the all-important, metaphorical door.

Ewa was clearly one of those 'connectors' we introduced in the last chapter: a person who not only has lots of contacts who feel positively towards them and are willing to help but also – and this is crucial – is prepared to share those contacts unselfishly with people whom they trust not to abuse them.

While it's true that 'if you don't pay, you can't play', focussing on formal networking opportunities and switching your networking radar on and off to the exclusion of chance meetings and informal conversations can mean that you miss a lot of opportunities. Let's consider two modes of networking activity: 'hunting' and 'gathering', or to put it another way, 'targeted' and 'diffuse' networking.

When we're in hunting mode, we have a pretty good notion of what our quarry is and a pretty good idea of what we're going to do to track it down. If you're looking for a new job, you probably know what you want to do, in what sector and even with which company, which allows you to put out 'feelers' to people who you think might be able to help open some doors for you. For many people, hunting is their default mode, most of the time.

Other people are much more prepared to indulge in a type of behaviour more akin to foraging in the woods for whatever berries, fruit, mushrooms and herbs they happen to come across. In networking terms, this means meeting people with no pre-determined agenda, and exchanging whatever information seems interesting at the time. Chatting, even gossiping.

Networking isn't just about pitching up at networking events.

Please don't take away the idea that one mode of networking is somehow right and the other wrong. They're both right, and we all need to balance the two. What we're arguing for here is three things:

1. If your default mode is 'hunting', you need to be more prepared than you generally are just to catch up over a drink or coffee. It's interesting that it is often the more self-important individuals who object that they can't spare their valuable time on something so apparently lacking in purpose. However successful such people have been to date, operating in this fashion is like being a top tennis pro who has a superb baseline game that compensates for being weak at the net. How much better could even a good player be by improving their net game rather than compensating for it? Remember the case study about Chris Ingram in Chapter 1? Despite his success, he couldn't predict when he might need help in a hurry.

2. If you view asking for help or a favour as a sign of weakness, you really do need to change your attitude. Nowadays, nobody (and we mean *nobody*) possesses all the information and resources they need to do their job or live their life. We all without exception need a little help, and asking for that help is simply recognising and dealing with reality. Learning to ask for the right help from the right people at the right time is a skill which we should all develop.

3. All of us should probably be prepared to do more of both than we typically do.

If you need convincing of the value of the 'let's just see where this conversation might go' approach, the following case study might help persuade you.

CASE STUDY

Smile And The World Smiles With You

Nyssa, a Chinese student in London, told us this story:

"I was working part-time on the check-out at my local Tesco to help fund my studies. I'm a friendly sort of person, and I like talking to people. I don't have any agenda – I just like people! So it didn't take me long to become friendly with many of the regular customers.

"One day, a customer asked me what I was going to do after I graduated. I told him that I wanted to stay in the UK for a while and get some real-life marketing experience here. Instantly, he told me that his company was looking for marketing staff. He sent me the information and I managed to get a job there. All through being friendly (and, I hope, having useful business skills)!"

So we would argue that you need to acquire the networking habit. Networking isn't something confined to crises in your life (when you're job-hunting, for instance) – nor should it be restricted to formal 'networking' contexts. Ask any smoker about networking, and they'll instantly tell you that one of the best places to network is with other smokers, on the pavement outside the building. The smokers all have an addiction in common that crosses all corporate boundaries – so the MD may find himself chatting to the office manager, an IT expert talking to a salesperson. If you don't smoke, don't start; but do remember that making time to exchange a few words over the water cooler or while you're making coffee is time well spent. And if you're a member of senior management, you'll probably already know that chatting to staff informally is probably the single most effective way of finding out what's really happening in your company.

IN A NUTSHELL

Acquire the networking habit.

There's another good reason, however, why we think it's so important to be prepared just to meet and chat, and that's to do with other people's impressions of you. If the only time they ever hear from you is when you want something, we really don't need to spell out how that makes you look in their eyes. And if you keep asking, without giving anything back, then sooner or later they are likely to stop being helpful. We're not for a moment talking about anything so crude as keeping score of favours, but if you're not open to hearing about what they're doing, how they're getting on and where they might like to go next, you'll have no way of helping them out with contacts or information unless they ask you directly – which people are often reluctant to do. There's a body of academic research that looks into why people don't ask for help when it would clearly be in their interests to do so, with reasons including:

- **Not wanting to owe someone a favour**

- **Not wanting to look needy, helpless, powerless or incompetent**

- **Not thinking to ask**

- **Not knowing who to ask.**

Here we come to the core issue of 'giving' versus 'getting' as a philosophy of networking life. One of the grounds on which networking is sometimes criticised is that it is manipulative and all about getting other people to do things for you. We want to say as loudly as we can that we firmly believe that this approach to networking is short-sighted and counter-productive.

Here's a very personal case study that demonstrates why we believe that giving can ultimately be more useful than getting.

CASE STUDY

Judith Helps Out

Steve, a colleague on the Sloan Fellowship at London Business School, was writing the business plan for a handheld tourist guide

as part of his Master's thesis. Back in the late 1990s, the concept of a handheld device that would help you find your way around (via GPS technology) and then also give you local information was pretty revolutionary.

Steve, a practical sort of guy, had got the technical side of things all worked out. What he didn't have was content – but he knew whom he wanted to partner with (Dorling Kindersley, a well-known publisher of illustrated travel guides, among other things), and he knew where to go for help in finding an introduction: me!

 "You used to work in publishing," he said. "Who can you introduce me to at Dorling Kindersley?" "Nobody," I replied instantly. "I've never worked with them." But then I thought for a moment, and remembered that I'd heard on the grapevine that David, with whom I used to work at Cassell, had moved to Dorling Kindersley. I also realised I could easily make a phone call and find out if I was right.

I was easily connected to David, who was intrigued by Steve's project and was happy to refer him to the right person internally. Since we hadn't been in touch for a while, there was quite a bit to catch up on. I mentioned that one of my reasons for going back to university was to change direction, and that I was extremely interested in branding.

"Aha," David replied. "Why don't we meet up for a chat?"

The end result? Steve collaborated with Dorling Kindersley, wrote his thesis, and got his degree – although his business didn't materialise (clearly, it was well ahead of its time). And I got my first job after business school as Brand Development Director at Dorling Kindersley. All because I made a single phone call to help a friend out.

Key to this case study is the fact that Judith had no ulterior motive in mind. She was simply happy to help Steve out, and had no idea that Dorling Kindersley wanted to develop their brand. The favour cost nothing but, in the end, serendipity gave a royal payback. Of course we aren't suggesting that, each and every time you do someone a small favour, the benefit will be as enormous as the job that materialised in this example. That would be ridiculous. All we're saying is that we all need to give more, and expect less in return.

We said in the last chapter that, to coin a phrase, 'the rich get richer'. So if you're seen by your peer group as someone who is prepared to offer your help, your contacts and your time, you develop a reputation as a lump in the porridge of life – someone about whom others are likely to say "Talk to X: he/she knows lots of people and is always happy to chat." Developing such a reputation doesn't just mean responding to requests – it means actively seeking out ways to help.

IN A NUTSHELL

"Ask not what your network can do for you; ask what you can do for your network" (with apologies to John F. Kennedy).

We've talked about formal networking opportunities and the benefits that accrue from simply meeting existing acquaintances just to 'catch up', but there's a third source of networking opportunity that you can harness, and that's luck. But surely the whole definition of luck is that it's random? Well, yes and no...

We agree that, if you throw a dice, choose a card from a shuffled deck or pick a number on the roulette wheel, then the outcome is down to chance. But that's a very different thing from luck. After all, is someone who carefully follows 'form' and gets a great return from a bet on the horses or stock market 'lucky'? Is Warren Buffet merely lucky? We might want to think so, but a slightly envious 'they get all the luck' attitude discounts or ignores the time and effort that that person has put into making themselves 'lucky'.

What we're driving at is that there are certain behaviours that seem to help make people lucky – and those behaviours can be unravelled, codified and reproduced. If at this stage you doubt the importance of luck, study the biography or autobiography of almost anyone whom society considers successful. Or read the following case study.

CASE STUDY

Against The Odds

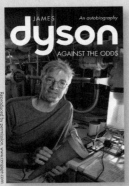

Oswald Jones and Steve Conway (from Manchester Metropolitan University and Aston Business School) studied the autobiography of James Dyson, serial inventor and entrepreneur.

In their study, Jones and Conway pinpoint the many factors that, together, help to explain Dyson's success. Not surprisingly, the usual suspects of good ideas, persistence, hard work and self-belief come high on the list. In addition, there's the not-unexpected help and support of close family and friends.

More interestingly for us, though, Jones and Conway emphasise time and time again the crucial financial, legal, business and emotional support provided by the weak ties that we introduced in the previous chapter. These included:

■ A lawyer friend of his brother-in-law helped Dyson to set up his first company, producing revolutionary wheelbarrows.

■ The lawyer was so enthusiastic about the product that he convinced Dyson's brother-in-law and other in-laws to invest in the company.

■ A former beauty queen friend was roped in to tour garden centres, promoting the wheelbarrows.

■ A respected businessman, who was also an old friend of Dyson's father, was persuaded to add gravitas to the company by joining the board.

■ Key to the success of Dyson's next venture, the bagless vacuum cleaner, was a Canadian he had sat next to on a plane. The fact

continued overleaf

continued from previous page

that they just happened to be reading the same novel by Fay Weldon proved to be the first building block of a firm friendship. This fellow Weldon fan ultimately headed up Dyson's North American operation.

- Lacking capital to set up vacuum cleaner production in the UK, Dyson approached a supplier with whom he had had a profitable relationship back in his wheelbarrow days, and with whom he had stayed in contact.

- Dyson studied at the Royal College of Art in London and always maintained his links with the college. When he needed the input of fresh, young graduates to make sure that his product incorporated all the latest technology, his contacts at the RCA were able to suggest suitable candidates.

- Dyson's old tutor from the RCA designed his new UK factory as the company outgrew its original home.

- Last but not least, Dyson opened an Australian subsidiary though a truly chance connection – someone who had seen a presentation he had made in Wisconsin called him up, wanting to collaborate.

To quote Jones and Conway: "Without these [social] networks it is unlikely that Dyson would have overcome what were no doubt formidable odds."[1]

We've presented this case study in some detail to give you a taste of the sheer variety of contacts that proved helpful. So don't underestimate the importance of contacts made on planes, in business meetings and seminars, or in your early career or education. You can never, ever predict...

Part of the explanation of this phenomenon lies in research carried out by people like Richard Wiseman, Professor of Psychology at the University of Hertfordshire. Wiseman, who popularised his academic research in his book *The Luck Factor*,[2] has carried out practical experiments to help determine what makes some people lucky and

1. Oswald Jones and Steve Conway, *The Social Embeddedness of Entrepreneurs: A Re-reading of 'Against the Odds'*, Aston Business School Research Paper RP0023, September 2000.

2. Robert Wiseman, *The Luck Factor*, London: Random House, 2003.

others either less so or even downright unlucky. What he and others have found is that being 'lucky' is in part a state of mind and in part attributable to a set of behaviours that highly effective networkers seem to share.

The mindset aspect to being lucky might sound a bit weird, but there's some good evidence for this from a number of sound academic sources. The most interesting comes from a psychological metric known as 'locus of control' – in plain language, whether someone feels that they are in control of their own destiny. Those with an internal locus of control tend to view what they achieve, for better or worse, as down to their own actions and decisions, whereas those with an external locus of control will put down their successes and failures to the action (or inaction) of people or forces beyond their control. Research has found that people with a high external locus of control have more accidents than those with a high internal locus of control – suggesting that there is something about the way they interact with their environment that makes them demonstrably more unlucky.

If you don't believe that it's possible to make yourself lucky (or at least to put yourself in a situation where good things can happen), consider the following.

CASE STUDY

Sowing And Reaping

Rob, who attended a workshop at Aston Business School, told us:

"Back in 1992, I was made redundant from my job as a development engineer in a small electronics company. Over the next 18 months, I didn't manage to find another full-time engineering position, but I kept busy with various temporary jobs. I eventually ended up working as a machine operator in an embroidery factory, a job that I only got by 'not mentioning' the fact that I had an honours degree!

"My father had been the steward in a local working men's club for several years until 1990, when he took the lease on a public

continued overleaf

continued from previous page

house. In September 1993, Dad bumped into George, one of his old customers from the club. During their conversation this gentleman asked after me (I had worked part-time at the club during university vacations). My father proceeded to tell George the story of my redundancy, etc... George's response was to tell him that the engineering test facility where he worked was looking for an engineer. George handed over the relevant contact details – and armed with this information plus a referral from George, I rang up and succeeded in arranging an interview. One week later I had got the job and started work!

"The job turned out to be a really challenging one, and it gave me masses of good experience. As a result, I've been able to move to Jaguar, into management and on to an MBA at Aston."

At first sight, this is just a nice coincidence. But isn't that what luck is? Rob was 'lucky enough' to:

■ Not be too proud to take a job for which he was over-qualified. One wonders whether his father would have been so willing to put in a good word for his son if Rob hadn't been so determined.

■ Have made friends with people he came into contact with (specifically, here, people he served during his holidays; but, having met Rob ourselves, we're pretty sure that he generally makes a point of being friendly and easy to talk to).

■ Get on well enough with his father to be able to tell him what was (and was not) happening in his life.

■ Seize an opportunity that presented itself by making contact with George to find out about the job and ask for a personal referral, and then ring up the company in question.

■ Realise that 'luck begets luck' and learn the important lesson that giving can be as good as, if not better, than getting. Rob in turn did a good turn for the authors of this book by giving them a referral to his later employers!

Purely blind luck? Or partly luck and partly building a supportive network and grasping each and every opportunity that presented itself? It's not just racehorses that wear blinkers: every one of us does in various ways, and one of the biggest conceptual obstacles that we encounter when trying to help people network effectively is the recognition that a straight line is not necessarily the shortest distance between two points.

DO TRY THIS

Point To Point

Draw two points anywhere on a sheet of paper. What's the shortest distance between them? Is it the straight line you've drawn between them? Actually, no it isn't: the shortest distance is made by folding the piece of paper so that the two points actually face each other and are in direct contact.

Now dust off that old school atlas, find a map that shows the northern hemisphere and draw a line to show the shortest distance between London and Los Angeles. A straight line? Again, no it's not, because that map squashes the curvature of the earth on to a flat surface and distorts it, so the shortest distance would, on that same map, look like a curve (technically a 'great circle').

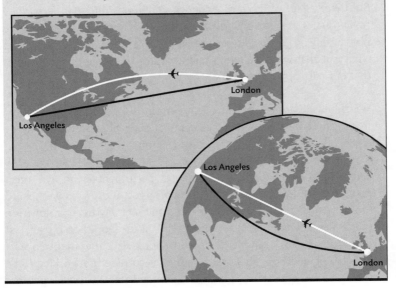

What we're trying to get across here is that truly effective networking demands a willingness to look laterally and creatively at possible ways to connect with individuals or jobs and to recognise – and grab – serendipitous opportunities when they come your way. Sometimes, what should be a direct and productive route gets you absolutely nowhere while a fortuitous encounter or a long shot produces immediate and spectacular results.

IN A NUTSHELL

Think laterally and creatively about who might be able to help you (and vice versa).

Making your own good luck is certainly part of the equation, but what role does personality play in all this? Even without knowing any of the theory surrounding the so-called 'Big Five' personality traits of extraversion, agreeableness, conscientiousness, emotional stability and openness introduced by Eysenck[3], you can imagine how the interplay of these factors will contribute significantly to an individual's innate networking propensity, ability and efficacy.

But there's a lot of research evidence to demonstrate that personality traits usually change very little over time, and very slowly. So if we're not modifying personality in the space of a one-day workshop, just what is it that we are altering that accounts for some of the changes that our participants report?

We think the answer is that our approach is to consider networking from a functional viewpoint, as a set of skills possessed innately by some, but which can be modelled and learnt by others.

Anecdotally, we know that workshop participants who get most immediate benefit fall broadly into two camps: those who we help to 'do it' better (that is, they understand the strategy but fall down on the tactics and execution) and those who, at the workshop outset, just don't 'get it' (for example, they fail to appreciate the importance of networking and how networks operate, or consider networking to be somehow beneath their dignity). So it immediately becomes apparent

3. Hans Eysenck, *The Biological Basis of Personality*, 1967.

how a well-designed and well-delivered workshop (or 'intervention', as it's called in the academic literature) can help change the 'actions' of the first group and the 'mindset' of the second without making any claims to affect their underlying personality.

Now that you know the rules of the game, how do you put them into practice? Let's start, in the next chapter, with ways of breaking the ice when talking to new acquaintances.

CHAPTER FOUR

Breaking the Ice

90% of success is turning up.

WOODY ALLEN

'Working the room' is a phrase common in the political and business community, which has probably done more to harm the reputation and concept of networking than any other: it implies manipulation, using people and engaging them only for what you can wring out of them.

We've probably all encountered that sort of false networker – who greets you warmly but drops you like the proverbial hot brick when they decide that you haven't got anything they want. Do any of us really want to be seen as that sort of person? Of course not, and while this chapter will certainly help you put yourself across as Mr / Ms Sincerity, you'd be missing the point (and perhaps missing some rather interesting – or even life-changing – opportunities) if that's all you want out of it.

What we're really trying to do here is create a change of mindset that:

1. Encourages you to engage with people for what they have to say rather than what they can offer

2. Helps other people to respond positively to you

3. Recognises that the most interesting relationships, opportunities and introductions can spring from the most unlikely beginnings.

In short, you need to appreciate that meeting new people is fun. Not just useful or interesting, but simply enjoyable. And before we go any further, just a reminder that much of what we're talking about in this chapter is just as applicable to 'one-on-one' interviews, meetings and purely social situations as it is to the 'cocktail party' environment that many people naturally associate with the term 'networking'.

In some respects, networking is very much like gambling: if you don't pay, you can't play. And to take that analogy a little further, you don't know in advance which bets will pay off and which won't; but, as we'll see, there's a lot you can do to stack the odds in your favour! At this stage, don't even stop to think whether the payback is a business opportunity, a new friend or just an interesting chat that doesn't actually lead anywhere...the crucial but incredibly simple starting point that gets missed by so many people is that to network you need to be able and willing to open conversations.

Networking means talking to people!

But how many of us really do that day to day? The answer is "Not as many as you might think". When for instance, was the last time you had a meaningful conversation with someone you didn't know?

CASE STUDY

A Visit To The Opera Pays Off

Kay, an MBA student at London Business School, told us:

"I used to work in London for two real estate investment management firms in business development and marketing. A couple of years ago, I was at an industry conference in Vienna. At the time I was working for a start-up firm and got chatting to Anne, who was a Director of Business Development for a large global firm – in other words, right at the other end of the spectrum of my industry.

"We found that, as well as having a lot in common professionally, we were both interested in art and culture, and were keen to see more of Vienna. Anne told me that she planned to spend the weekend after the conference exploring; I recommended the production of Carmen that I had just seen at the Vienna Opera House, and told her about some easy ways to get tickets. We also exchanged ideas about other things to see. We ran into each other again the next day, both having left the conference early to pop into the Kandinsky exhibition across the way.

"Nearly eight months later I was at a cocktail party in London hosted by the same association that had run the conference

continued overleaf

continued from previous page

in Vienna. The start-up I was working for was failing and the office was closing; I was to work there for just one more week. My company (and its imminent demise) was the topic of many conversations, and I was speaking to a lot of people about what was going on. As the evening was ending, I spotted Anne and asked her if she had enjoyed her weekend in Vienna after the conference. She immediately thanked me for my advice about the Opera House and we got to talking. When she learned that my employer had fallen apart, she invited me to lunch the following week... and offered me a job working for her several weeks later."

Just a straightforward encounter? Certainly, but there are some interesting learning points:

1. It was entirely Kay's decision as to whether or not to fully engage Anne in conversation the first time they met. She could have made polite small talk about the world of real estate and left it at that, as so many people do. Instead she engaged fully, and gave as well as got information. What would you have done?

2. Look at how much Kay and Anne learned about each other through one conversation and another chance encounter. As well as professional links, they quickly found out that they had a lot of cultural interests in common, too.

3. See where that chance conversation led. Not immediately, but later, when Kay really needed help. Just luck, chance, fate...? Or keeping one's eyes and ears open, engaged and receptive?

But what about you personally?

DO TRY THIS

What's Your Attitude To Chance Conversations?

I strike up conversations with the person next to me on the plane/train/bus.

Always   Often   Sometimes   Never

In a queue, I'll talk to the person in front of or behind me.
Always   Often   Sometimes   Never

If in a shop, I'll chat to the shop assistant.
Always   Often   Sometimes   Never

Even if I'm just having a casual chat, I really listen to what people say, and try to engage with them fully.
Always   Often   Sometimes   Never

If someone tries to open a conversation with me, I respond positively.
Always   Often   Sometimes   Never

How did you score? Now, repeat the exercise but this time, try and come up with a specific example in each category, and jot down anything you can remember about the conversation; what did you learn about the other person? Clearly there are times – such as when entering a negotiation – when it's useful to be able to engage someone in conversation very naturally as a means of gaining important information without appearing to be 'pumping them'. Here's a real case study that makes the point.

CASE STUDY

Tony Goes House Hunting

My wife and I were hoping to buy a house, and we were interested in River House, although we'd noticed that the estate agent seemed rather unwilling to discuss the vendor's situation. Coupled with the fact that the house didn't feel quite as 'lived in' as one would expect, we had the distinct feeling that there was something we were not being told.

Before our second viewing of the house, we stayed the preceding night in a guest house a couple of doors away. On arriving, the proprietor conversationally asked us what we were doing in the

continued overleaf

continued from previous page

area. There followed a desultory discussion about house prices generally and the information that "River House on the corner there is for sale, but it's pretty expensive", and the rather more interesting information that the proprietor's understanding of the asking price was £25,000 less than we had been told by the agent.

The next morning, we were again chatting to the proprietor as he brought in our breakfast. On the question of crime, the area was pretty good, he said, with the minor exception of occasional nuisance with druggies hanging out down by the river: mental note #1 for us. "What about flooding?" we asked, knowing that what was true of the guest house would also be true of River House two doors away. "I've been here twelve years, and the worst I've seen is the water come up to within three feet of the top of the bridge's central arch, but when the river does break its banks, it spills over the low ground to the south, so that protects the houses along here": mental note #2.

"So what's the story with River House? After what you told us yesterday we had a look at the details in the estate agent's window." "Now there's a story," said our newfound friend. "Lady who owns the house works in the village. Son lives there too...he's pretty harmless. But the husband's been a bit naughty...seems he was on the financial side of a number of companies and skipped off with £73 million of their money." Mental note #3 to make absolutely sure that there was clear title to the property if we were to proceed. It certainly explained why the estate agent was a bit cagey, and might help from a negotiating standpoint if the vendor was under pressure to sell.

There are actually four quite distinct elements in this interchange:

1. The simple fact of being prepared to open a conversation with a stranger (it's here, of course, that many people don't even get out of the starting blocks)

2. Finding or creating the right opportunity to get that conversation started

3. Choosing the right opening words

4. Steering the conversation in the 'right' direction (assuming there is a 'right' as opposed to 'wrong' direction, which isn't aways the case).

So let's go right back to square one and analyse the process of engaging someone in conversation. If you're one of those people who find it difficult, do remember that what seems to come naturally to some people only does so because they've learnt those skills – almost certainly unconsciously through family, education or upbringing. The tips we present here are exactly those that anyone who might be termed 'socially confident' uses, and they can be learned by anyone. But, like any newly acquired skill, they need practice to develop them and keep them honed.

Just to remind you before we get into this, there are four recognised steps to mastery of a skill – think about your experience of learning to drive or ride a bike:

1. Unconscious incompetence: you don't know what's involved in doing something, because you've never been exposed to it

2. Conscious incompetence: you now know what you want to do, but you don't know exactly how

3. Conscious competence: you've learnt to do something, but it takes every ounce of concentration to do it

4. Unconscious competence: you can do it with your eyes closed; it has become second nature and you don't need to think about what you do.

Moving 'up the ladder' from unconscious conversational incompetence to unconscious conversational competence takes time and effort. But once you get there, meeting and talking to new contacts will seem as easy as falling off a bike. In other words, you'll wonder why you ever found it difficult and be surprised at how enjoyable is; the effort will definitely be worthwhile.

Many (if not most) people are too reserved or self-absorbed to start a conversation, so you'll often need to take the initiative.

To illustrate the various skills involved, let's take a step by step journey through the thing that so many people find so difficult: the typical 'networking' event in which you have to walk into a room full of people you've never met before and engage someone in conversation.

The first thing to remember is that the event doesn't exist in splendid isolation. Somebody organised it, and there's probably a guest list that might be available in advance if you asked for it (and most people don't ask, so the simple fact of asking could give you an easy advantage). Of course, some organisations won't share that list. It may be a knee-jerk reaction to being asked for information, or they may think that being the pivot point between participants gives them power. But asking for – and getting – that guest list does at least allow you to research those people and companies that you might be interested in meeting.

Even if the advance guest list is beyond your reach, the chances are that there will be a table laid out with name badges. So why not arrive early and take a look at those badges – or at the guest list that one of the organisers is bound to be carrying around with them. Short of walking around the room peering hopefully at people's name badges, however, how do you go about connecting with that person whom you really want to meet?

CASE STUDY

Tony And The Needle-Free Injection

While a student at London Business School, I was invited to the annual drinks party of a city corporate communications outfit that I knew handled the PR for several pharma, biotech and medical device companies. At the time, I was on the prowl for three things: freelance work to help keep my head above water while doing my Masters, a possible project for my thesis and a post-Masters job.

I knew that among my host's clients was a company that specialised in needle-free injection technology – a concept that appealed enormously and potentially ticked all of the boxes above. I also knew that the company's CEO was on the guest list, but never having met him before or even seen a photo, circulating hopefully among several hundred people at a City venue didn't seem like a very useful strategy for tracking him down.

Instead, I arrived early, looked over the badges neatly laid out on the reception table and noted where his badge lay. Keeping one eye on the desk, I watched my CEO arrive and pick up his badge. I now knew what he looked like and how he was dressed, making it easy for me to approach him later in the evening and introduce myself.

As it happens, nothing came of that encounter (at least in part because, in the white heat of the first term at business school, I don't think I followed up after the event) but we had an interesting conversation and I learnt a lot about the technology from someone I probably wouldn't have met if I had left things to chance.

While on the subject of name badges, they exist for a reason, and here we make a plea to all event organisers everywhere: What is the point of creating name badges on which the type is so small that it is unreadable from a normal interpersonal distance? And why book an expensive venue and then give people cheap badges with safety pins designed to ruin a decent jacket or dress? That sort of badge only encourages people to wear them somewhere where they won't do visible damage – which means wearing them somewhere they can't be seen. Does that matter? Human psychology says it does.

Mike's Very Special Ski Hat

I noticed a photograph on Mike's bookshelf: him in full skiing regalia, wearing a woolly knitted hat bearing his name in big letters across the front. "What's the story behind this?" I asked. Mike smiled and said: "My mother knitted me that hat. Whenever I wear it in the ski lift queue, people talk to me. When I wear an ordinary hat, it's as if I'm invisible!"

Not wearing a name badge at formal events can deter people from approaching you.

So, wearing a clearly visible, easy-to-read name badge can encourage other people to approach you, taking away the burden of having to make the first move. Don't put your badge in your pocket or hide it under your jacket.

The next step is to find someone to engage in conversation. But who? First of all, why not just look for a friendly face. Chances are, if someone actually makes eye contact with you and smiles, they're not going to give you the cold shoulder if you approach them and the people they're chatting to. It may seem obvious, but it does work.

Another tactic is to make your way across the room to the bar or buffet table. Not only does that give you something to do but very often you can fall into conversation with someone else who is debating whether to go for red wine or white wine, or should they stick to juice? "Have you tried the white? Is it drinkable?" Not the most devastating opening line, but nevertheless a perfectly good way to start a conversation. As is "Those nibbles look nice!" or "Not sure how I'm going to manage to eat that without dribbling it all over myself!"

However, if the sea of faces you're confronted with is, at best, indifferent, then what next? We wish we could give you 100% foolproof advice about what to do next. Reality dictates, though, that we can't. What we *can* do is help you avoid falling into 'elephant traps': that is, stumbling into really uncomfortable situations.

The most straightforward tactic is probably to find someone else who is standing on their own, because the chances are that they will welcome you warmly. Nobody likes standing by themselves. A participant in a recent workshop turned this idea on its head, by saying that he always tried to arrive at events early. "Doesn't that mean that you're often standing alone, in splendid isolation?" we asked. "No," he replied. "When the room is still pretty empty, it's quite acceptable to be standing by yourself... and the very fact that you're a singleton encourages people to come over and start a conversation."

The other alternative is to find two or more people standing together and see if you can join their conversation – but how to do it in a way that makes you engaging rather than aggressive, and without stopping the existing conversation dead in its tracks?

We've all heard the oft-quoted saying: "You don't get a second chance to make a good first impression". Bearing that in mind, let's take a detour into some important aspects of body language.

The fact is that when people are really engaged or absorbed with each other, they generally (and unconsciously) adopt a 'closed' stance. If the group is just a pair, they tend to stand roughly parallel to each other; if more people are involved, then the group forms a rather 'closed' circle or triangle. In this situation, the participants have effectively declared an 'exclusion zone', which makes it physically more difficult for another person to join them. Just look at these drawings.

CLOSED STANCES

If, on the other hand, you watch people who are meeting for the first time or having a casual chat with a friend or acquaintance, you see a very different picture. Look at people chatting in pubs, clubs, parties and networking events, and you'll see that time and time again they adopt a more 'open' stance, which approximates to 120 degrees. As you can see, there is physically space for another person to approach and join the group.

OPEN STANCES

What these two very different physical stances signal highly effectively is the mental preparedness of the participants to include someone new in the conversation. And what that means in practice is that you can spot from across the room those groups that are less likely to welcome you and more likely to make you feel uncomfortable (because they are signalling 'keep out' with their bodies). We've noticed, anecdotally, that when just two people are in conversation, they are more likely to get deeply involved in the conversation and so adopt a relatively closed stance; in contrast, larger groups tend to be, almost by definition, more open. So a quick glance around the room as you enter can be enough to send you in the right direction.

IN A NUTSHELL

Body language is a powerful indicator of people's state of mind. Use it to avoid falling into uncomfortable 'elephant traps' at networking events.

At this point, you might well ask what to do if the one person in the room whom you really want to chat to has got that mental 'keep out' sign on show. Of course, you can choose to ignore it or decide that everything we've just said is rubbish; but be warned that physical posture is usually a really good indicator of mental state, so even if you're received civilly and politely, that person is likely to be less than optimally receptive to your approach. Far better to bide your time, wait until their body language signals 'open for business' and make your approach then.

A word on manners here might be appropriate. The (often unconscious) signals that we send out via body language are very powerful. Even in the 'safe' environment of a workshop, most people feel extremely uncomfortable when asked to role play these 'keeping out' and 'letting in' postures. That, of course, is a good thing: we want people to leave our sessions more sensitised to the way the world works. Turning all this on its head, though, it's crucial to remember your own manners and, if someone approaches your group, make a point of welcoming them aboard. There's no need to make a song and dance about it – just a quick smile or nod of recognition, or a slight shuffle to one side to make room for the newcomer is all that's needed. For all you know, that person may turn out to be the most interesting person you meet all evening!

DO TRY THIS

Mind Your Manners

Next time you're at a networking event, or a conference or just an informal party, make a point of being friendly to people you don't know. You'll be amazed at how responsive most people are.

Once you've selected whom you'd like to approach, the most direct way to proceed is just to go up to the group, try to catch someone's eye, offer your hand and introduce yourself. That might sound aggressive, but done delicately and with due regard to body language to ensure (as far as you can) that they're not having a private discussion, it can be a very quick and effective way of joining a group.

continued overleaf

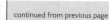

continued from previous page

How do you invite yourself in? You'll have to find a form of words that works for you, but "Do you mind if I join you?" will do for starters. There's the risk (albeit very small) that some joker will reply "Yes, we do", so you might prefer something that doesn't even offer a way out. "Hello, I don't recognise any faces here, so I thought I'd introduce myself. I'm John Smith" might sound rather contrived or wooden when you see it in print, but it's the sort of opening that works well in practice as long as it's done without implying that you want to take over the conversation.

In case you think we're over-simplifying, here's an example of how important self-awareness is.

CASE STUDY

Tony Helps To Create A Smaller Splash

During a workshop, I was approached by a participant, who said he always had great trouble joining groups. I was rather surprised, as the person concerned was physically large, imposing and highly extrovert, and dominated the room with his presence. I would have expected him to have absolutely no trouble introducing himself to new faces so, to try to get to grips with his problem, I suggested we 'mock up' an introduction to see what happened.

And suddenly I could see it: his sheer physical presence plus his degree of extroversion meant that his arrival in a group of people and his 'planting' of himself in their midst killed any existing conversation stone dead and destroyed the previous dynamic of the group. The picture I instantly got in my mind's eye was of a large man entering a swimming pool full of sedate swimmers by 'bombing' them rather than using the steps or a neat dive.

The interesting thing is that the individual concerned had absolutely no idea of what he was doing wrong – only of the effect of large physical size coupled with extroversion. Once we'd (tactfully) unpicked the problem and shown him how to tone things down, the effect was transformational.

You might say that such a 'full frontal' approach just doesn't suit your style or personality. But, before you discard the idea, at least be prepared to try it at one or more events where there's not too much at stake. Like so many of these techniques, they get to feel more natural and relaxed with practice. And remember that, even if you feel self-conscious, the chances are that no one else will notice.

What we like to call 'linger, listen and launch' is probably the most commonly used technique. This uses the psychological quirk that, if you stand with a group for a while, listening to the ebb and flow of the conversation but without actually introducing yourself or participating, you somehow get accepted as a 'member' of that group without even having opened your mouth. By the time you feel ready to contribute something (and you really do have to make a contribution, otherwise people will eventually start wondering why you never say anything), you won't be an outsider even though you never asked to join. Once you've made a contribution, you then have an opportunity (if you choose to take it) to follow up immediately with something along the lines of "By the way, I didn't introduce myself; I'm Jenny Jones."

A third line of attack is to hitch a ride. An event's hosts or organisers are supposed to look after their guests, so do feel free and within your rights to approach one of them and say "I don't know many people here – I wonder if you could make some introductions?" Similarly, if you spot a friend or acquaintance, ask them to help you out. Phrased tactfully, this is effectively giving them a compliment. As well as being receptive to flattery, almost all of us also like to help.

If you don't use the 'linger, listen and launch' approach, you now need to get the conversation started. The case study with which we opened this chapter involved using the location quite informally to initiate a conversation about the delights of Vienna. But you don't have to be somewhere as intrinsically interesting as Vienna to use the 'local scenery' as a 'hook' to open a conversation. It doesn't need to be actual scenery – it can be 'temporal' scenery, like something that you've both just experienced, seen or heard. The British, of course, are internationally renowned for talking about the weather – and what's that if not scenery? However, it's possible to be a bit more creative than that and an important point is that being creative in opening a conversation doesn't mean that we're being manipulative: we're just having a chat.

Tony Gets Knitted

It being a sunny day, I parked myself at an empty outside table at a café with the intention of grabbing a coffee and drafting a press release. As lunchtime approached, the restaurant filled up and eventually a woman approached my table and asked if she could occupy the empty seat. Of course I agreed, and went back to my work in splendid silence.

We must have continued in our own little worlds for nearly an hour and several coffees, with me filling up my notebook during this time and resorting to scribbling on the back of receipts from my wallet. Eventually, having run out of available surfaces to fill, it suddenly occurred to me to lean over and ask my table companion whether she'd let me have a couple of pages from her notebook.

She kindly obliged, but nothing more got written down as, having opened the conversation, Jane and I got chatting and had a wide-ranging conversation that must have lasted another half hour. Jane had just that day signed a publishing deal for her book about domestic handicrafts, and I specifically remember being introduced to the quite alien concept of 'knitting circles' that meet to knit on the Circle Line tube and in Foyles bookshop (among other places). Not in itself the most useful piece of information, but absolutely fascinating. When I explained what I did for a living, Jane commented that her husband worked in a senior position for a large corporate, and that his view was that all MBAs had roughly the same technical skills and that it was the interesting ones who got the job.

So, not only did I have a fascinating conversation with a very engaging lady, but I unexpectedly learnt something anecdotally useful about how the corporate world views the MBA. All that from asking for a piece of paper. I still have Jane's business card some three years after that encounter, and I see she now has three titles in print and a fourth due out soon.

Just to show that the process can work in both directions, here's another case study in which Tony was on the receiving end rather than acting as initiator.

CASE STUDY

Tony, The Tecchie Traveller

I tend to write not on a PC or laptop but on a PDA linked to a folding Bluetooth keyboard. One reason is that I find it easier to write when away from the distractions of my desk, and I prefer not to lug a laptop round with me if I can avoid it. But the PDA/folding keyboard combination remains an unusual one, so removing the components from one's pockets or bag and assembling them into a workable word processor often attracts a fair bit of interest.

We were in Florida for a friend's wedding, and I was taking advantage of some time off by the pool to work when a stranger stopped at my table and expressed wonder at my computer set-up. I explained how the various parts went together, that it was nothing he couldn't buy for himself, and that I was working on a book about networking.

It turned out that Jim (we'd done the introductions by this stage) was a realtor from Ohio who fully appreciated the importance of networking and was keen to see the end result of my labours.

From that point on, I bumped into Jim on most days of our stay, discovering that we were the same age, had sons of much the same age and a divorce each into the bargain, amongst other things. Over a year later, Jim and I are still in email contact, and the promised mention of him as a Case Study on just how easy it can be to strike up a conversation with a total stranger has come to fruition.

Jim, you're famous.

We've said all along that networking isn't just about talking to people at large (or small) 'events'. If you're having a one-to-one meeting at someone's office, keeping your eyes open can tell you a huge amount about them that you ignore to your detriment. If you've ever had to conduct a meeting in a totally characterless 'meeting room', you'll know how difficult it is to do anything other than get down to business. Take this anecdote, for example.

CASE STUDY

Judith's Himalayan Encounter

I had arranged to meet Jane, Head of Learning and Development at a major firm of accountants, and was wondering how to break the ice. After all, the aim of my meeting was, to be blunt, to sell our workshops to her. And if networking is about building relationships, so is selling!

As I was shown into Jane's office, my problem was instantly solved because right above her desk was a gorgeous framed photograph of snowy mountains. "That's beautiful", I said. "Did you take it?" The instant reply was "Yes, I did as a matter of fact. Thank you. It's Annapurna."

And we were off – talking about mountains and snow, trekking and the Himalayas. I personally love trekking, but don't like altitude, so I was interested to hear her advice about low level trips to the Himalayas.

By the time we got round to talking business, we were, if not firm friends, then at least good acquaintances. By establishing rapport with Jane I had, inadvertently, shown her that I could connect with participants in my workshops. Jane liked me, and was much more inclined to buy from someone she liked than someone to whom she was indifferent.

If Judith hadn't looked around as she was ushered into a very impressive corner office, she might not have noticed the photograph – and would have missed a golden opportunity to get the encounter off to a good start. In order to use the local scenery, you have first to be aware of its existence, so developing the facility for 'active looking' is an important enabling skill.

DO TRY THIS

Silent Witness

The next time you find yourself cooling your heels in a waiting area, bar or café, have a look round at the other occupants. Choose one and think about how you'd go about approaching them to introduce yourself. What local 'scenery' is there? Is there anything that they are doing that could provide a 'hook' for the conversation (an interesting book, a gadget)? Is there any shared experience you could use (a delayed flight, a noisy environment)? How might you frame an opening remark to that person?

There's another aspect of using the local scenery that presents a fantastic opportunity for meeting new people but is often overlooked. On more formal occasions, the organisers often provide some form of roaming entertainment: magician, juggler, living statue, balloon sculptor or similar. Have you ever stopped to wonder what purpose they serve? Chances are that the phrase on the tip of your tongue is 'ice breaker' or 'to give people something to talk about'. But next time you see one of these performers at an event, indulge in a spot of people watching. How many people miss a golden opportunity by stopping their conversation to watch the performer, clapping politely and then resuming their conversation. Instead, why not turn to someone you've never spoken to before immediately afterwards with a comment such as "Great trick...any idea how that was done?... By the way, my name's Gloria Stitz." And you're into a conversation with almost no effort.

IN A NUTSHELL

The scenery is there to help you, so use it.

Granted, it's not always easy, or even possible, to create these openings, but the mental process of looking for them is what we're trying to inculcate here. At events, conferences and parties, things are usually that bit easier because everyone knows that the whole point of being there is to talk to other people. But even then, we risk carrying our mental baggage with us:

Judith Learns A Valuable Lesson

At London Business School, I got very interested in branding, and managed to get myself on the invitee list for a series of presentations put on by Interbrand, a leading light in the world of brands. As I walked into the reception before my very first event, I truly felt outnumbered, outflanked, even outclassed. Everybody, I was certain, was more sophisticated than me and more 'in the know'.

I clutched my drink, and told myself sternly that I ought to find somebody to talk to. But before I had time to really panic, a be-suited man walked up to me and said: "You look like you know as few people here as I do!"

Once I had overcome my surprise, I replied that I didn't know a soul, and that led us to inquire how we each came to be there. And then I had my second surprise. This chap turned out to be a director of Marks and Spencer. So he wasn't a sad person who had no connections. He was a very important person, who simply didn't know many of the people who happened to be in that room.

The encounter taught Judith a valuable lesson. She was thinking that, because she didn't know anybody, she herself must be nobody. Whereas this man simply took things at face value: 'I don't know anybody here so I'd better set about meeting some of them.'

So next time you find yourself among strangers, remind yourself that your attitude is all-important; the glass needs to be half full, not half empty. A room full of strangers is an opportunity, not a threat.

Five Corners

Michael, who attended a presentation to the Shell Women's Network (yes, men are invited too!), told us this tale:

> "A shy friend of mine shared her method for dealing with intimidating networking events. She simply uses her father's simple rule. As a bishop, he has to attend lots of functions and often needs to remind himself to circulate, rather than get too involved in individual encounters. How does he do this? He simply makes sure that he always meets five new people: someone from the middle of the room, and someone from each of the corners. Simple but effective."

If this sounds impossibly daunting, here's another tip that might help.

In The Post Office

Practice really does make perfect, but it's best to make mistakes when failure doesn't matter too much. So next time you're in the queue at the post office or the supermarket checkout, have a go at starting a conversation with the person behind or in front of you. Or with the waiter at a restaurant or café. You'll be amazed, we promise, at how quickly you get better at this. Soon it'll become second nature – so that when something important is at stake, you'll feel calm, collected and confident.

The next step, of course, is turning that preparation into action, but we're not going to invite you to do that until you've read the next chapter because, having opened a conversation, the challenge is then to keep that conversation alive and create a feeling of mutual involvement or 'rapport'. And rapport is such an important topic that it deserves, and gets, a chapter all to itself.

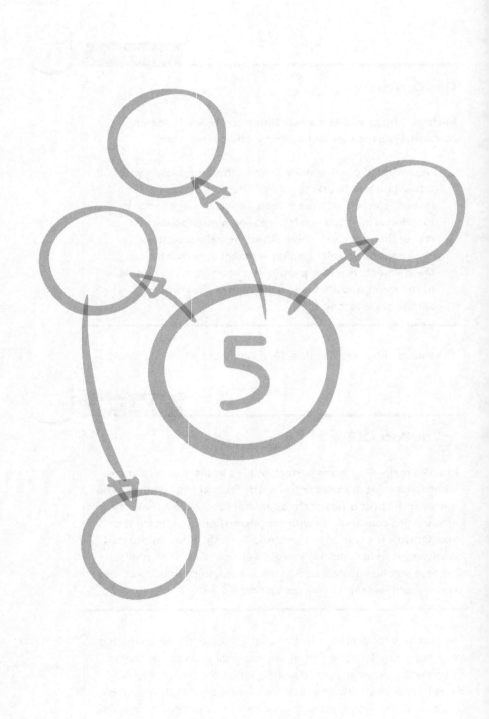

CHAPTER FIVE

A Question of Rapport

*Pull the string, and it will follow
wherever you wish. Push it, and it
will go nowhere at all.*

DWIGHT D. EISENHOWER

What is it that makes one person 'click' with another? Why do some people become firm friends and others remain cool and distant with each other? What makes people interested in each other?

These are huge questions, and we certainly don't claim to have all the answers, but in this chapter we'll look at some very specific things that you can do that should help improve the likelihood that other people will find you an entertaining, interesting and useful person with whom to network. After all, networking is about relationships of all kinds – from the merest acquaintance to the closest friend – and what all of these have in common is (varying degrees of) rapport. Without rapport, your relationship with someone is rather like a name on a database – interesting, but not necessarily productive.

IN A NUTSHELL

Building rapport is one of any networker's most important tools.

The material we're going to cover here breaks down quite conveniently into three sub-headings, all of which fit together to create a psychological jigsaw called 'rapport'. Let's define rapport as a sense of mutual trust and respect, a feeling of empathy or harmony between two (or more) people. In other words, a sense of getting along well, which you can foster through:

- **How you look**

- **What you say (or don't say)**

- **What you do.**

We'll deal with these in order. But before we do, can you think of a time when you made an instant decision that you disliked someone...or that they disliked you?

CASE STUDY

Mistaken Identity

We were running a workshop at the University of Edinburgh Management School and had just briefed participants on an exercise, the object of which was for pairs of people to try to find two or three things they have in common. Since we wanted to mix people up a bit so they weren't just working with their buddies, we decided to pair students up randomly rather than let them form pairs themselves.

As the group reconvened after the exercise, two girls were giggling exuberantly. It turned out that they had been on the same MBA programme for over six months. In all that time, they had never talked to each other because, as one of them put it, "she looked 'stuck up'". That sentiment of course conveyed itself to the other protagonist through body language and avoidance mechanisms, leading to a situation in which two people disliked each other for almost no reason at all. Only when forced together accidentally on our workshop and made to communicate – and specifically required to find some common ground – did these two women realise the mistake they had made. Had they not been thrown together in a networking workshop, they might have disliked each other to this day.

Clearly, first impressions can be hugely important. Even before we open our mouths, others are forming impressions about us based not only on our appearance but also on their own preconceptions and mindset. The fact is that our brains are hardwired to identify patterns and to make the best predictions they can, based on prior experience. It's the trap those two girls fell into before we unintentionally dragged them out of it.

While we can't do a lot about people's preconceptions (except be aware that they may exist), it's relatively easy for us to control the way we look. We've all been in situations where we've (possibly unwittingly) found ourselves 'wearing the wrong uniform'. It's uncomfortable, and generally avoidable. Perhaps more interesting is the situation where a relatively small change in your dress can make a huge difference to whether you are accepted (or not), as the venture capitalists in the case study below knew very well.

Judith Learns About Dressing For The Occasion

I was making a presentation to the annual get-together of a niche venture capitalist. They had around a dozen start-ups under their wing, and once a year they brought the entrepreneurs, their directors and non-executive directors, and senior staff together. Understanding the value of networking, they wanted this diverse group of people to meet and learn from each other.

When I mentioned the importance of first impressions, my contact, Stuart, intervened, to tell everybody an anecdote. In the brave new world of the early 2000s, dress codes were much more relaxed than they used to be, and many of the men in the office didn't bother with a tie. However, they all kept a spare tie in their desk drawer, 'just in case'. If formally dressed guests arrived, it was the receptionist's job to give an advance warning, enabling them to up their own 'formality rating' by at least wearing a tie rather than an open-necked shirt.

Much as they all hated wearing ties, the staff of this VC were well aware of the importance of dressing appropriately and following accepted dress codes.

So it's worth thinking consciously about how you want to come across, and making sure that the impression you project is congruent with the one you intended. The other side of this coin is the fact that it's all too easy to pigeonhole someone based on their outward appearance and so take the interaction no further – potentially missing out on all sorts of interesting relationships and information. Listen to your instinctive response, by all means, but beware of snap judgements.

But what should you talk about? It's a crucial question, because this really is the point at which others will decide whether or not they want to have a conversation with you. Perhaps the single most important point to remember is this:

IN A NUTSHELL

Most people are more interested in themselves, and the things that motivate them, than they are in you.

We do realise that this may be stating the case a little too baldly. And, yes, we also realise that there certainly are people who are genuinely interested in hearing what others have to say (and they are, in all probability, naturally effective networkers). But before you get depressed about human nature, let us ask you a question: could you regard this 'self-absorption' as helpful?

We think the answer is 'yes', and our reasons are very simple. First, it means that, to be an effective networker, you don't have to be an unabashed extrovert. You don't have to shine and sparkle; what you need to be able to do is draw the other person out, and get them talking. And second, doing that isn't too difficult – the quickest route to creating a good impression is to ask good questions and listen actively to the replies.

The reason lies in a human failing: we are all susceptible to being paid 'psychological compliments', a concept echoed elsewhere in this book. The reason that asking someone good questions about themselves pays them such a huge psychological compliment is that it basically says "I am interested in what you have to say and I want to know more" or even "You know more about this subject than I do; I'd like to learn from you".

Another manifestation of the psychological compliment is in asking for help and advice: it's amazing how generous people will be with their time and knowledge if you make them feel that they know more about a subject than you do. Letting them feel superior is a much better way to get someone 'on your side' than constantly trying to 'trump' them, as so often happens in testosterone-fuelled conversation.

Which all leads on to the issue of good and bad questions.

A good question is one that opens up the conversation, potentially takes it in a new direction and gives the respondent the opportunity to expand on some point. Bad questions just close everything down – useful in a power play perhaps but not for effective networking. Crucially, a good question (and a good conversation) relates to material that the respondent is interested in talking about.

Often, in business or professional situations, we allow our conversations to get bogged down in business or professional subjects. In trying to impress people with our expertise, knowledge and experience, we forget that beneath the job titles and status symbols lies a host of hobbies and experiences, many of which have absolutely nothing to do with our work.

IN A NUTSHELL

People have more than their business cards in common.

What do you do when you're not working? Are you equally comfortable chatting about your work or your outside interests? And if you met someone at an event with the same interests would you rather talk about these or work? So why should it be any different for anybody else?

CASE STUDY

Finding The Way To San José

Emma, a senior manager with Shell UK, told us that she is naturally an introvert, and used to struggle to generate the rapport necessary to influence her superiors and colleagues in other parts of the organisation.

A while back, Emma wanted to get support for a forthcoming project from a member of the executive team whom she barely knew. She mentioned the fact to a colleague, who happened to be a good friend of this person. The colleague advised her: "Try this. She has a hideaway in San José, where she goes to de-stress. Tell her I said 'Hi', and ask her if she's been to San José recently."

Emma's initial conversation with the woman from the executive team began fairly formally. But when Emma asked her about San José, she collapsed in a chair, saying "Actually, I was there last weekend with all the people who are very important to me to celebrate my birthday..." After a lengthy and quite personal chat about life, work and everything in between, she then asked Emma: "So how can I help you?"

The tone and content of the subsequent business conversation was changed irrevocably – for the better.

Emma clearly had a lucky break in finding someone who could throw her a valuable pointer on how to find out what mattered to this woman, and says she learned a lot from the experience. Specifically:

■ **Even senior managers have insecurities and passions, and it's crucial to find ways of reaching out to them**

■ **Even if you're under pressure of time, look for the personal**

■ **If one approach doesn't work, try another. Emma's normal manner is very focussed and solution-orientated. It's taken her a while to readjust to a more relaxed style to connect better with senior leaders.**

In some situations, of course, the main tie that binds is work. But in other situations, and with other people, it may be their outside interests that make them tick. Finding out about those interests and chatting about them can be a great way to create rapport and deepen a relationship.

What Floats Your Boat?

Next time you find yourself with someone you only know through work, create an opportunity to ask "What do you do when you're not working?" And see how the conversation – and the relationship – opens up.

Taking this a step further, is it best if this leisure interest is different or shared? The answer is both. Talking to someone with interests or experiences outside your own gives you the opportunity to use networking to learn about other people, other businesses, other professions, other neighbourhoods, other countries...the list is literally endless. Networking becomes a way of learning about the world, of exploring and expanding your horizons. We talked, in Chapter 1, about the "social origins of good ideas": it's these we're referring to here.

In fact, we'd go so far as to say that, if you really can't find anything at all in common with somebody, then your relationship is probably doomed. If we, literally or figuratively, speak different languages and aren't interested in learning about each other, then it will be an exhausting, uphill struggle to build a firm foundation for an acquaintanceship, let alone a friendship.

On the other hand, finding common ground with someone creates an almost instant and automatic bond. In fact, searching for commonality is one of the simplest ways of building rapport. And it's almost always possible. As we've already mentioned, we regularly get participants in our workshops to chat in pairs, looking for things they have in common. Only on one single occasion, out of all the many workshops we've run, did a pair of participants fail the exercise! As you'll see later, that was for a very specific reason.

The list of possible things that can link people ranges from the most important to the most trivial, from the general to the universal. Take travel, for instance. You may both simply enjoy travelling, and like hearing about new places to visit. Or you may have visited the same country, or even city – in which case, there'll be plenty of specific stuff to talk about, as you swap horror stories or share recommendations. In case you're stuck for ideas, try one or more of the following headings: place, pastime, plans, pets, pathology, position, project, politics, possessions, profession, progeny...

Here are some actual examples culled from our workshops:

■ **Two people discovered they had undergone exactly the same surgical procedure, in the same eye**

■ **Colleagues found out that they had lived in the same London suburb at approximately the same time**

■ **Sometimes, it takes more cheek to find that something. For example: Question: "Have you ever been in the navy?" Answer: "No, I haven't." Response: "Well then, we have something in common. Neither have I!"**

■ **At a small company that had to manage global clients, an Italian salesman talked of his difficulty in engaging with a Japanese client. Until, that is, he inadvertently asked him about his flight – and unleashed an unexpected (and shared) interest in things aeronautical.**

All this is easier than you might think. The link doesn't have to be important; sometimes trivia can work just as well, as the following case study suggests.

CASE STUDY

An Unexpected Link

When they first met, nobody really expected George W. Bush and Tony Blair to get on. But look at this extract from the first press conference they gave:

Question: There has been a lot said about how different you are as people. Have you already in your

continued overleaf

White House photo by Eric Draper

continued from previous page

talks found something maybe...some personal interest that you have in common, maybe in religion or sport or music?

Bush: Well, we both use Colgate toothpaste. (*Laughter*)

Blair: They're going to wonder how you know that, George. (*Laughter*)

The point we want to make with these examples is twofold.

1. Almost anybody can find something in common, if they want to, and

2. That 'something' doesn't have to be hugely deep and meaningful. But, on the other hand, if it does matter to you, so much the better, as this next case study shows.

CASE STUDY

A Meeting Of Minds

Early on in her career, Sarah worked for a well-known multinational. Jack, a senior manager, was scheduled to visit the UK and, as a relatively junior member of the team, she was given the job of 'baby-sitting' him. In other words, it was up to her to take care of the logistics, and to make sure that Jack got to all his meetings with minimal hassle.

The advice she was given was unambiguous: "Jack's very senior and a bit of a workaholic so stick to talking about work and don't push yourself forward too much."

Sarah managed to follow this advice for a couple of days but, she said, the whole task became unutterably boring. So much so that she decided to throw caution to the winds and try to engage with Jack on a more equal basis, as one human being to another.

"The transformation was miraculous," she said. "Jack opened up instantly, and we had some really good conversations. What was pretty amazing was that we very quickly discovered that we're both absolutely passionate about food. I'd been lucky enough to take a course at Rick Stein's Seafood School – and Jack was envious as hell!

"The rest of our time together was really enjoyable – and believe it or not, three years later we're still in touch."

So, finding things in common, and things that matter to both of you, is a double whammy.

As well as the subject matter of what you talk about, it's worth spending a moment on the way you phrase questions. There's a real skill in framing questions in such a way as to get a useful answer. Consider the following rather typical question at a networking event: "Did you enjoy the presentation?" To which an obtuse, unsocial, difficult or just plain lazy respondent could reply "Yes, I did" or "Not really". It's the sort of answer that doesn't take the conversation anywhere and puts the onus back on the questioner to ask something else; it's a closed question and can elicit a closed answer.

Courtesy of The Kipling Society

If you're ever stuck for a good question, here's a nice 'aide-memoire' from the *Just So Stories* by the British author Rudyard Kipling:

I keep six honest serving men,
    (They taught me all I knew);
    Their names are What and
        Why and When
    And How and Where
        and Who.

· R V D Y A R D · K I P L I N G ·

Change the semantics of the question very slightly (turning it into an 'open question') and you can completely change the outcome. If the question instead becomes "What did you think of the presentation?", the respondent is pretty much forced to give you some degree of qualification in their answer: "I really enjoyed it. The story about the balloonist was particularly interesting."

This at least offers more room for manoeuvre than the previous response. Of course, the respondent may be bloody-minded and still cut the questioner off at the knees by simply saying: "Yeah, it was good." But if that's the case it starts to look as if the respondent is being deliberately contrary or has a real social skills problem.

But asking good questions is only half the story; 'actively listening' to the answers is an equally valuable skill.

Answers are just as important as questions. However the question you ask, or are asked, is phrased, it's always possible to give an open answer, one that takes the conversation forward and gives the other person something to get hold of. Networking is a two-way street, and if you're going to network effectively and enjoyably, you have to give as well as take.

We've probably all encountered the individual who asks question after question but seems to take no great notice of the answers being given. Either the questions are so disjointed that you wonder whether your answer really matters, or the questions just keep coming with your own questions being batted aside or answered in a way that makes you wonder why the respondent is so anxious to throw the focus back on to you. The first experience is like being in a tennis match where you're just being served at again and again with no possibility of returning the ball; in the second, it's a match where you manage to return the ball but the opponent just ignores it.

Somewhere between these two extremes lies the comfortable, friendly rally that makes for a great conversation in which each side is actively listening to the other. Couched in these terms, the skills of active listening are self-evident. But that is by no means always true, as the following case study shows.

Only Connect

Almost without fail, when set the task of finding things in common, everybody succeeds in uncovering something. At one workshop, though, one participant raised his hand and stated in a clear and loud voice: "No, we couldn't find anything at all in common. Really there was nothing..."

Not terribly surprising. Steven (not his real name) was an uncommonly uncommunicative person. He had told us, right at the outset, that he wasn't sure of the value of all this networking and socialising stuff. He was there on sufferance, because he'd been told to attend.

More interesting, though, was the fact that, almost at once, his quietly spoken partner in the exercise spoke up. "That's not strictly true," he said, clearly irritated. "But you hardly asked me any questions, and just talked about yourself. So *I* know what we have in common, even if you don't!"

There's a moral to this story – asking questions is a sure-fire way of generating rapport, but only when you pay the person you're talking to the compliment of listening to their answers. When we chat to someone at an event, or as a precursor to the 'meat' of a business meeting, the truly effective networker recognises that this is not mere 'small talk', and that what we're actually being given is a window into that person's life: what they like doing, where they've been, who they know, what makes them tick. Apart from some great conversational opportunities, that information also gives you a excellent opening to follow up after the meeting and stay in touch by using the relevant and personal stuff you've learnt by active listening.

We're sometimes asked whether it's really legitimate to use this sort of personal material, and our answer is that of course it is, because what you're doing by using this personal detail is actually paying the other person a psychological compliment: you're saying "Not only am I interested in what you told me, but it stuck in my mind."

Shared Experience

When we run workshops, we often play a private game. As we learn about the participants, we try in our own minds to find something in common with each of them. As the day progresses, it's rare for us not to be able to latch onto something they say. Why not try the same thing next time you listen to a presentation, or attend a meeting. It won't always be hugely important to you; but as you develop the skill, you'll find you're able to find something in common with almost anybody.

But, asking good questions and actively using what you've seen or been told is not in itself enough to sustain a conversation. Part of the business of creating rapport comes down to making yourself accessible – and even vulnerable. And that means offering something about yourself and colouring your conversation with your own experiences.

It means being able to tell a good story.

CHAPTER SIX

And Who Are You?

Wit is repertoire.

OSCAR WILDE *(attributed)*

As we write this, we can almost hear the chorus of "But I'm no good at telling jokes!", "I don't like talking about myself" and "But nothing interesting has ever happened to me!", so let's get something clear about each of those excuses before going any further.

This is not about telling jokes. Jokes are one-way vehicles designed to be delivered to an audience and, more importantly, aren't usually things that have really happened to the joke teller. They don't encourage interaction of the "And what happened next?" or "How did you deal with that?" variety. While jokes certainly have their place in the cut and thrust of conversation, serial joke tellers can actually be extremely tiresome simply because of that lack of opportunity for interaction.

Countering the second and third objections will take up the bulk of this chapter. Even if you claim not to want to talk about yourself (and, tell the truth, isn't there a tiny bit of false modesty here?), you're going to have to learn to do so. We've all had conversations with people who simply refuse to tell you much about who they are or what they do. We usually emerge from such encounters feeling drained, literally pumped dry of energy. That's because, we would argue, any conversation or exchange between two or more people is literally that: an exchange. So, even if good conversationalists learn the art of being really interested in the person (or persons) they're talking to, they also know that they have to give of themselves.

Let's start at the very beginning. How do you introduce yourself? By that, we don't mean just the act of offering your name, but answering the spoken or unspoken question "And what do *you* do?", which often gets disguised and presented as "And how do *you* come to be here this evening?" The way you answer often sets the tone for where the conversation goes next because the conscious or unconscious subtext is often: "Tell me why I should want to spend my time talking to you." Or, even more bluntly, "Are you a useful person to know? Or an interesting person to talk to?"

So how you answer that question can make a real difference.

"And What Do You Do?"

Before reading on, grab a piece of paper and write down what you typically say about yourself when people ask you that question.

Of course it depends on context, and the first point to make about crafting a really good introduction is that it's emphatically about tailoring it to the situation, rather than taking a 'one size fits all' approach. Let's take a simple example of three introductions by the same person.

- "I'm a doctor."

- "I'm a doctor, and I run the allergy clinic at the local hospital."

- "I'm a consultant in clinical immunology specialising in allergic rhinitis."

While the first answer is entirely true, it also doesn't offer a lot of information. It may encourage the follow-up question "And where do you do that?" or "So what sort of doctor are you?", but there's also what we would call a 'mental full stop' at the end, firmly passing the conversational buck. It's almost as if you're telling them that, if they want to find out more about you, they're going to have to work for the information. Almost any answer that is just a couple of words long falls into this trap: I'm a lawyer, I'm an accountant, I'm a student. In each case, there's something extra that you could add, to help the conversation move along.

The second example, in contrast, gives a little more information and, we would suggest, implies that you're happy to have this conversation.

But while this answer might work fine in the context of the local PTA barbecue or the annual village fete, using the third variation in that same environment might come across as rather heavy handed or pompous – and not the way to get the best out of people. In contrast, it would be entirely appropriate as a means of setting out your credentials if the conversation were taking place at a medical conference.

What general principles can we extract from these examples?

First, its important to remember that, from a networking perspective, a good introduction doesn't start with you mentally stamping on another person but doing everything possible to allow the conversation to deepen and broaden. Even a hint of boasting or pomposity can kill a perfectly good conversation stone dead.

The opposite is also true, of course, as this case study shows.

James Passes The Buck

At our workshops we generally run an interactive exercise where participants have to introduce themselves and then give each other (constructive) feedback and criticism. James was quick to speak out.

"That's easy," he said. "When someone asks me what I do, I generally just reply: 'Oh, what I do really isn't interesting. Tell me about yourself.'" James sat back, obviously sure that he had made the right move, to be met by complete silence and some very confused expressions. "Why are you all frowning? What's wrong?" he asked.

Gail piped up and voiced the response of the whole group: "You can't do that!" she said. "It made me think that you really didn't want to tell me anything about yourself." And almost everybody else in the room murmured their agreement with Gail's verdict.

James's experience was a real eye-opener for him. He thought he was pressing all the right buttons – not trying to dominate the conversation, drawing the other person out and so forth. He was genuinely surprised, and disturbed, to discover the response that his carefully thought out introduction produced. So often, we don't realise exactly what effect our words have.

If you really are reluctant to talk about what you do, you'll need to find a more positive way of diverting the conversation. How about this? "I'm a lawyer by day, and play the trumpet by night." With luck, the next question will relate to you, the trumpet player rather than you, the lawyer.

And here's another real example: "I have three roles. I'm volunteer coordinator for alumni of Los Andes University living in London, I work for Centrica, and I'm the mother of a young son." As Diana told us, she decides which of the three to put first depending on the context and where she wants to place the emphasis.

So if you accept that your introduction dictates how the conversation unfolds, it's worth creating a good one (or rather, good ones, plural). If you don't rehearse at least roughly what you're going to say in any given environment, the chances are it won't come out quite right when you really need it. And if you don't try some of it out on a friendly ear, you might mistakenly give the wrong impression.

But what makes a good introduction? Having heard many examples (some wonderful and some excruciating), we think that there are a number of targets you should be hitting:

- **Do you sound as if you want to be there, talking to this person?**

- **Does it make you sound interesting?**

- **Does it come across as friendly and engaging?**

- **Does it make you sound like someone worth talking to?**

- **Is it appropriate to the context?**

- **Is there a 'hook' in there that gives the other person something to latch on to and continue the conversation?**

It goes without saying that every person, and therefore every introduction, is different. So it's virtually impossible to tell you exactly how to go about crafting that introduction, to make sure that it ticks all these boxes. But here are some pointers...

Don't say too much. People don't want chapter and verse, just enough to keep the conversation going. And don't say too little, either. People should feel that you want to tell them about yourself. You need to tread the golden mean between an overly long, two-minute elevator pitch (just try to talk about yourself for two minutes, and you'll see how long 120 seconds really is) and a single, abrupt phrase.

Avoid jargon (unless you're talking to another expert) – and this includes using your job title as a substitute for actually answering the question. "I'm a project manager" doesn't tell me very much, nor does "I'm a marketing manager for a large FMCG company". The following case study presents an extreme, fictional example of this.

CASE STUDY

I, Robot

If you've seen the 2004 film *I, Robot* starring Will Smith as homicide detective Del Spooner and Bridget Moynahan as Dr Susan Calvin, a robot psychologist who is more in tune with robots than human beings, you might remember this encounter:

> Detective Spooner: "So, Dr Calvin, what exactly do you do around here?"

> Dr Calvin: "My general fields are advanced robotics and psychiatry although I specialise in hardware to wetware interfaces in an effort to advance USR's robotic anthropomorphization programme."

> Detective Spooner: "So, Dr Calvin, what exactly do you do around here?"

> Dr Calvin: **"I make the robots seem more human."**

Dr Calvin's initial answer may be entirely accurate, but to most of us it was also entirely incomprehensible. So Spooner is forced to repeat himself in order to elicit a reply that he can understand and relate to. Back in the real world, when faced with this sort of reply most of us might (a) feel uncomfortably ignorant, (b) suspect that this person really isn't interested in engaging with us and (c) either repeat or rephrase the question (along the lines "So what exactly does that mean?") before beating a hasty retreat.

Here's an example of how you might improve a jargon-filled response.

CASE STUDY

Would A Ten-Year-Old Understand?

Craig's initial offering in a "What do you do?" role play was: "I'm a financial controller in BT, supporting the Group HQ directors and working on a project to streamline BT Finance."

Not surprisingly, his partner in the exercise found that extremely off-putting. Together, they crafted a sentence that didn't hide behind 'business-speak' and made Craig sound more approachable. The new improved version went like this: "I help BT save money by measuring us against the best in our industry and helping to improve things."

Craig was pleased with the result – and told us that he'd been struggling, just a week or two back, to explain exactly what he did to his young nephew. Now he felt much better equipped to find the right words.

While we're not saying that everything you say needs to make sense to a child, the lesson we can all learn from this example is that using too much technical language does nobody any favours. And that trying things out on a colleague can be very helpful.

The only exceptions to the 'jargon rule' might be if your job title is really unusual or interesting. At one workshop, a young man told us: "I'm an ideas apprentice!" The broad smile implied in that reply worked really well in so far as it tickled our fancy, and made everybody curious to know more.

That example leads us back to the delicate issue of jokes and, more generally, making people smile. While we're emphatically not suggesting that each and every one of you come up with a funny line to describe what you do, we are firmly of the opinion that, if you do make someone smile, you're well on the way to winning them over. Here are a few examples that we've heard in workshops:

- **I'm an accountant, and I love my job!**

- **I'm a rocket scientist.**

- **I help people spend money they haven't got...**

- **I'll give anybody advice about almost anything. It's usually called consultancy.**

- **I build skyscrapers.**

Remember, though, that if you make a quip or say something enigmatic, then you can pretty much predict that the next question will be along the lines of "And what on earth does that mean?" In other words, you still haven't escaped from the need to prepare. You can't (and wouldn't want to) script an entire conversation – but you can and should be prepared for obvious and expected questions.

DO TRY THIS

Horses For Courses

Now that we've made you think about the whole subject of tailoring an introduction, revisit what you wrote earlier in the chapter and compose versions which are optimised for:

- **A vacation encounter around the swimming pool**

- **An industry conference**

- **Your company's annual get-together.**

Then find a friend you trust, and try them out on him or her.

So, now that your handcrafted introduction stands a fighting chance of making someone genuinely interested in taking the conversation further, let's challenge the other cop-out we highlighted at the start of this chapter.

DO TRY THIS

The Art Of Storytelling 1 – The Examined Life

Go back as far as you like in your life and make a list of the most interesting, weirdest, funniest things that have happened to you, the most embarrassing and most uplifting moments. We call these things Fascinating Facts and everybody has some. It's just a matter of dredging them up from our memories.

To help you, here are some real examples we've come across:

■ I learned to ski at the age of 14. After only four days I won a bronze medal in a slalom competition.

■ Last summer I went cruising with five friends in the Mediterranean. Suddenly, and unexpectedly, our boat's engine caught fire and we were forced to abandon ship and had to wait an hour in the water till help arrived.

■ I have drunk meths with tramps in a Johannesburg park.

■ In 1997 I took a year off and travelled around the world alone.

■ I went water-skiing at midnight in Alaska.

■ I have published several articles on human mycoses.

■ I can find buried underground services using divining rods.

■ I swam with wild dolphins in Kenya.

■ I am the parent of twins and I am married to a twin.

continued overleaf

continued from previous page

- **I have made 12 parachute jumps, the first of which was a tandem skydiving jump 10,000 feet high by the Popocatepetl volcano in Mexico.**

- **I can build dry stone walls.**

- **I had my pilot's licence before my driving licence.**

You'll see that the variety is endless: anything from who you are to what you've done, to what was 'done to you'. If you're having difficulty, then perhaps the following subject headings will jog your memory: your work, holidays and travel, childhood experiences, unusual skills or hobbies, friends and colleagues, your home, your family...

There's almost certainly something there that you could talk about, but the next objection we have to handle is that you don't think anyone will be interested in hearing about it. Granted, your experiences may not be headline news, but by sharing them you're making yourself accessible, encouraging rapport and allowing the conversation to take off in new directions, as people chip in with "That reminds me of the time..." or "Something similar happened to me when...".

Which brings us neatly on to the two key skills of the conversational storyteller: how to tell a story which has a beginning, a middle and an end; and how to find a way to drop that story into a conversation in a way that fits in with the flow of conversation up to that point.

If you think this all sounds a bit stilted and contrived, then before we go any further we'll appeal directly to one of literature's greatest wits and raconteurs, Oscar Wilde, who was admired for always having the 'bon mot', the right word at the right time. But Wilde himself is reputed to have said, as we quoted at the head of this chapter, that "Wit is repertoire".

CASE STUDY

I Wish I'd Said That!

We have to come clean about the 'Wit is repertoire' quotation, not least because it's a nice example of a network springing into action to provide information.

When we came to check all the attributions for this book, nowhere could we find confirmation that Oscar Wilde had indeed said (or written) it.

So Tony sent a 'cold' email to Nigel Rees, presenter of BBC Radio's long running *Quote... Unquote* programme, asking for help. Back came an email from Nigel saying that he couldn't find any such attribution in any of his many reference sources which included the Osar Wilde Society. And that, thought Tony, was that.

Several months later, the following email arrived out of the blue:

Tony,

You asked about this earlier in the year and wondered if it was Oscar Wilde. One of my sleuths in the US has turned up a rather more likely source – an American actor and raconteur called Wilton Lackaye (1862–1932), of whom I had never heard before. If you click on the links, you will see why we think this is the man.

Regards,

Nigel Rees

How nice to discover that Nigel's network had quietly been gnawing away on this particular bone with no further input from Tony, ultimately yielding a result. And how gratifying that a busy man like Nigel Rees should have bothered to make the effort to 'close the loop' after so many months with a correspondent who was (to him) ultimately no more than a name and an email address. Hugely impresssive.

But back to Wilde (or whoever actually said it). What he meant was that the best lines were carefully rehearsed beforehand but only delivered when the occasion presented itself.

We can learn both from Wilde and from conversationalists who use the same set pieces in many different situations. Watch any chat show and you'll soon realise that the celebrity guests usually know exactly which anecdote they're going to use – as indeed does the host, who will often prompt with something like "Remind us of the time when you...", and the guest is off at a gallop with a story that delights the audience but has been told a thousand times before.

Our job here is not to turn you into professional raconteurs but to help you think actively about what you say, and the way that you say it.

To avoid turning into the sort of shaggy dog story that has people wondering how much longer they have to keep listening, the ideal conversational story has a beginning – the situation in which the speaker, or someone the speaker knows, found themselves – and an ending that resolves that situation. In the middle is the meat of the sandwich, which provides all the flavour and makes it real and engaging to the listener. To illustrate this, here's a story told by our colleague Cliff Dixon about something that happened to him a while back.

CASE STUDY

Cliff Goes Overboard

"On the penultimate day of a sailing holiday I was about to step off the boat with the bow line in my hand when I slipped on the anchor (new deck shoes and shiny soles) and fell on the edge of the concrete quay – hugely painful, but I was unsure of the extent of the damage.

"It being October, my charter flight the next day was the last of the season and I was determined to get home to England and to NHS treatment. The alternative was a six-hour ferry/bus journey to an Athens hospital. So I put up with the pain and swelling overnight, did the 'wounded soldier' bit at the airport at both ends to get a ride on a buggy with yellow flashing lights and got home via plane, train and taxi. I finally made it into my local hospital on the Monday morning to be told by the Accident and Emergency doctor 'This is very nasty – why on earth didn't you come to us sooner?'

"The degree of 'nastiness' was such that I spent four nights in hospital, not all of it down to the injury: I was wheeled down to theatre and back again twice before actually having the operation because a couple of road accidents were given greater priority.

"I ended up with pins and a plate in my ankle, and was in plaster for about four weeks. So life really can change in a split second."

What can we pull out of that one anecdote? First, it's rather engaging – you really do want to know what happened next. There's a sense of tension building up and release at the end. Second, the middle is full of detail that makes the situation come alive to the listener: something reminiscent of what we said earlier in the chapter, and it becomes obvious that what gives a story flavour is the "what, why, when, how, where, who" as Kipling's Six Serving Men make a return appearance.

The third thing about this story that we know but you don't (yet) is that Cliff has told this same story to many different people and at many different times – so in that respect it is a well-rehearsed set piece, but that doesn't detract from its power to engage.

And this brings us on to the second plank of conversational storytelling, which is how to insert one of your 'set pieces' into a conversation without it looking like a complete *non sequitur* that has your listeners wondering whether you've even been listening to what's just been said. It's a skill that requires you to think on your feet, and often think laterally, but mastering it can expand your conversational range – and the opportunity to create rapport.

Here are some general themes from Cliff's story:

- **Broken bones**

- **Sailing**

- **Holiday mishaps**

- **How travel arrangements can be so time sensitive.**

And here are a few that are actually work-related:

- **The need to deal with this issue quickly, before it becomes a crisis; things can go from bad to worse so quickly**

- **How important it can be to be assertive**

- **How best to deal (and not deal) with an unexpected event.**

You may think that anecdotes taken from our private lives can have little relevance to work-related networking and interaction. We would argue that you couldn't be more wrong. The examples we gave earlier can, with a little ingenuity, be used to illustrate quite a few very different business-related themes that could lead into that particular story:

- **Our staff have a multitude of talents, and can rise to almost any challenge. If I could do XXX, then surely we as a group needn't be put off.**

- **Don't tell me I can't do it. Let me tell you a story about something you'd never believe I could do...**

- **Perhaps we need to think laterally, try a different approach. For example, when I...**

- **It pays to try to prepare for the unexpected, as far as possible. For instance...**

- **Deal with things as they happen; don't plan ahead for every possible eventuality. Things usually turn out OK in the end. Did I ever tell you about the time when...**

- Careful planning really will pay off. I learned that the hard way when...

- We don't need years of experience. We're all quick learners; when I...

- What seems impossible at first glance is often perfectly possible.

- Let's trust our gut feelings, rather like I did when...

DO TRY THIS

The Art Of Storytelling 2 – Take It From Here

Starting with one of the interesting things from your own life that you identified earlier in the chapter, use the "what, why, when, how, where, who" model to craft that incident into a story that lasts a minute or two. Then think about and list all the ways that you could link into that story, both in a social and a professional context.

IN A NUTSHELL

If you don't sound interesting, why would anyone want to talk to you?

Making good conversation is important, but it all goes for nothing if your listener feels that your body language implies that you're not really engaged with them. So here we come to the role of non-verbal communication and body language in the creation of rapport.

We saw in the last chapter how people's posture differs unconsciously according to whether they are absorbed in a conversation or not, and it turns out that there are other unconscious behaviours we exhibit when we are 'in rapport' with someone. Knowing what those behaviours are can not only ensure that we are sending out the right signals (or not sending out the wrong ones) but also help us to gauge how well others are responding to us.

If you indulge in a spot of people watching (and we heartily encourage you to do so), the most obvious behaviour you'll see between people who are 'in rapport' is a more parallel or 'face to face' stance, which in effect puts up an invisible barrier that discourages others from joining the conversation. You'll see the same effect whether they're sitting or standing, and you can even see it on a park bench, where people will corkscrew around in their seats to face each other.

A more subtle clue to the degree of engagement or rapport is known as 'mirroring and matching'. If you watch two people in rapport, their posture is probably similar. In other words, they might both be leaning back in their chairs, or both standing with their arms crossed. And if you see one of them make a gesture, such as scratching their ear or crossing their legs, you may, a few seconds later, see the other person make a similar gesture, totally oblivious to the fact that their own action has actually been triggered by someone else. The point is that these unconscious responses signal that "I am in rapport with you", and the very fact that they are unconscious show just how powerful and basic these signalling behaviours really are.

IN A NUTSHELL

People who are getting along well tend to mirror each other's body language.

As well as helping us to recognise rapport when we come across it, body language can also help us to create that sought-after feeling of empathy. Simply by mirroring what the person we're trying to get along with is doing – adopting a similar posture, following their lead in making gestures – we can encourage the person we are in conversation with to feel more at ease.

Some words of caution here. First, we aren't advocating falseness and lying. All we are saying is that you can short-circuit and encourage the process of rapport building. And second, a little goes a long way, especially for the inexperienced. Too obvious or too crude mirroring may turn into mimicry and that will create exactly the opposite effect to the one you're aiming for.

CASE STUDY

A Little Done Well Is Better Than A Lot Done Badly

A nice and probably apocryphal anecdote concerns a salesman we'll call Brian, who had taken his lessons in mirroring too much too heart. He was talking to David, his 'prospect', and assiduously tried to mirror his posture and gestures. Done badly, it was all too transparent – and eventually David's irritation overcame his natural good manners.

Leaning back in his chair, David ostentatiously propped his feet on his desk and snapped at Brian: "Go on, why don't you f***ing mirror that!"

Needless to say, Brian didn't close the deal.

Not only did Brian not make a sale, but he left behind a poor impression, and David was unlikely to welcome him back. Which brings us neatly to the all-important question of ending conversations. Having made a real effort to engage in lively conversation, the last thing you want is to be inadvertently rude when you take your leave.

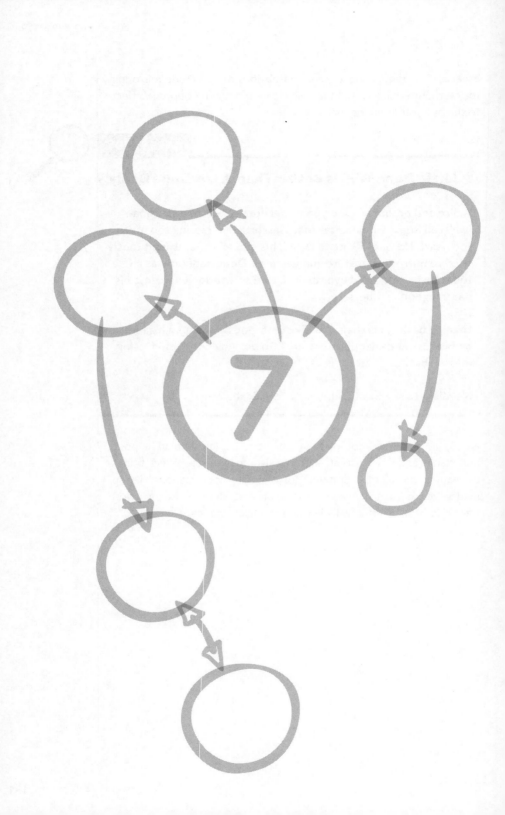

CHAPTER SEVEN

Hello, I Must Be Going

Breaking up is hard to do.

NEIL SEDAKA

At first glance, it might seem rather strange to dedicate a whole chapter to the business of closing conversations, but at pretty much every workshop we run, we're asked how to do this effectively. The scenario goes something like this: one person tells us about an experience of finding themselves stuck with someone at an event or party, unable to get away, and then almost everyone else in the room laughs or murmurs their agreement. It's clearly a very common problem, but why is it so universal, and what can one do about it?

Let's first deal with why this issue is so important in networking terms.

We've already acknowledged how important first impressions can be, but we sometimes forget that the impression we leave someone with at the end of a meeting or conversation can be just as crucial. What a shame and a waste to spend time and effort building rapport only to mess it up by letting a conversation or meeting go on longer than it should do, simply because you don't have the right tools to end it cleanly and comfortably.

It's embarrassing to both parties to find that they have run out of things to say to each other. Of course, the fact that it's hard to develop a really meaningful conversation in what may be a noisy and crowded environment doesn't mean that there isn't common ground, and the possibility of becoming friends as opposed to just acquaintances. 'Small talk' gained its name for a good reason, and it can be difficult (if not impossible) to take a conversation much beyond basic politeness in such circumstances.

IN A NUTSHELL

Last impressions can be as important as first impressions.

It's often at the tail end of such conversations that we trip ourselves up and say the one thing that we never intended to let slip, or switch inadvertently into 'selling' mode by saying that we're looking for a job, available for consultancy projects or have a fantastic investment opportunity. And, as we've said elsewhere, when you start selling yourself, the shutters tend to come down – just reverse the positions and think how you feel when someone starts trying to sell you their skills or their products.

Looked at from another perspective, if you can't end a conversation, then you can't move on to meet other people, make other contacts and expose yourself to new information.

Waiting until a conversation is dead on its feet has another major downside, rooted in the non-verbal communication that we've already said is so important to our social interactions, and that's the classic problem of 'cocktail eye' and 'cocktail ear'. You'll almost certainly recognise the scenario: you've been chatting with someone but the conversation is getting a bit mundane and you find yourself either starting to glance around the room wondering who to talk to next (cocktail eye), or half-listening to the conversation going on in the group behind you (cocktail ear) because that sounds so much more interesting than your current one. Either way, the message you send subliminally (if you're doing it overtly, then it just looks rude) is that you're no longer interested – and the moment you do that, you've probably lost that person's goodwill.

Here's an example of how powerful that effect can be.

CASE STUDY

Tony's First Date Is Almost His Last

Getting back into the dating game after a divorce isn't easy, so when I finally met someone I really wanted to ask out, I planned the event with military precision, booking the restaurant and deciding which bar had the right ambience for a pre-dinner drink.

Unfortunately, my military planning turned out to be seriously flawed, as I discovered that the bar I had chosen so carefully was closed that evening for a private party.

continued overleaf

continued from previous page

We made a bee-line for another bar, which was bursting at the seams, with nowhere to sit and standing room only at the bar. Not wanting to tow Jill around Covent Garden in a possibly fruitless search for a less crowded bar, and given that we were only having a drink before dinner, I decided that standing at the bar was the lesser of two evils.

Thinking that it was hardly chivalrous to keep a lady standing, I kept an eye out as we chatted for a table or a couple of bar stools to become vacant. What I didn't realise was the effect this was having on Jill, who interpreted my wandering eyes as a complete lack of interest in her or our conversation.

Only when a couple got up to leave and I immediately pounced on the now vacant table did she realise why I'd been so apparently inattentive. So rude had I inadvertently appeared that, had the table not become vacant when it did, Jill was apparently on the point of making an excuse to end the date there and then.

Jill and I have been married for over ten years, but only very recently did she tell me about this 'sliding doors' moment that could have ended our relationship before it got going.

The moral of the story is to keep your attention focussed on the person or persons you're talking to until you or they are ready to bring the conversation to an end. But the rather fortunate ending to this story signals another aspect to the cocktail eye/cocktail ear scenario, which is that, if you really do have to have a roving eye (for example, you're waiting for someone specific to arrive, or you're on the organising committee and need to ensure that food and drink is circulating efficiently), then you can neutralise its power to offend simply by telling the person you're talking to what you're doing and why: "Apologies if I appear to be looking round the room all the time, but I just need to make sure that people are being kept supplied with food and drink."

But how to bring a conversation to a timely and effective conclusion?

The fact is that we are rarely faced with anyone terminally boring: more usually, it's just a question of moving on before the conversation begins to flag. The difficulty is that, if you wait until the bitter end, you've already let yourself down because you're leaving at a low rather than a high. One of the hallmarks of an effective 'face to face' networker is an ability to move on effortlessly without appearing rude, bored or disinterested. To learn their secret, let's look at ways you can extricate yourself from a conversation.

The first is so widely used that it's become almost an accepted code for the fact that the conversation is at an end. "I'm just going to fill my glass" or "I'm just nipping to the loo" might actually be the truth, but from a networking perspective, think for a moment what message it sends to the person you've been talking to if they spot you thirty seconds later deep in conversation with someone else. The unspoken message you have sent them is:

1. You were not polite enough to tell them to their face that the conversation was at an end.

2. You actually told them something that was at best an excuse and at worst a downright lie.

3. You didn't have the courage or confidence to tell them the truth.

So, even if you both know the meaning of the 'toilet' or 'refill' code, it's a gambit that makes you look pretty weak and it's hardly the mark of an effective networker. To add insult to injury, if you're in a one-to-one conversation, it means leaving your 'partner' alone – a situation none of us like to be in. At the very least, why not note that both your glasses or plates could do with a refill and suggest that you both go over to the buffet. Almost invariably, you (or your partner) will fall into conversation with somebody else, and you separate almost without realising what's happened.

The next option involves actively being a connector, as described in Chapter 2. Instead of simply trying to get away from one conversation, why not try to initiate another one in the process. You could do yourself (or the person you're talking to) a good turn by potentially extending your (or their) network, as well as building your image as someone who really understands what networking is all about, and is willing to give and receive introductions.

In short, you could try one of the following:

- **"Can I introduce you to anyone here?"**

- **"Do you know so-and-so? I'd really like to meet him/her."**

- **"Have you met my friend John/Jane? I think you might have a lot in common."**

If neither of you know anybody else in the room, then you could 'invite' a third party to join your group simply by adopting an open posture and making eye contact with someone who might be hovering, or looking for someone to talk to. After a few minutes, you can then quietly take your leave. Alternatively, you could suggest that your little group latches on to another, offering something along the lines of "Shall we see where these guys come from?" Having merged the groups, you again quietly take your leave with nothing more than a "Nice to meet you, do excuse me" that doesn't interrupt the conversation.

Another approach is simply to be direct, polite and positive. While the words will differ, the common thread is that the 'leaver' manages to convey the fact that they've enjoyed chatting, but it's now time for them to move on. Because they've been 'straight' about their intentions, the person or people left behind don't take offence. With luck, they'll also have used their active listening skills to throw in a psychological compliment.

To illustrate what we're getting at, consider the following:

"It's been really nice chatting to you, but as this is a networking event I suppose we should both do some circulating. Could I have your business card and when I get home this evening I'll dig out the name of that wonderful restaurant we visited in Tuscany and send it on to you in good time for your trip."

This achieves a number of crucial things:

1. It says definitively that the conversation is at an end.

2. It conveys the idea that you should both be moving on rather than it being a one-sided departure.

3. It revisits the content of the conversation (in this case the proposed Tuscany trip), showing that you have actively listened.

4. By offering a restaurant recommendation, you have opened the door to a relevant and useful follow up in which you are giving to, not taking from, your new contact.

At this point, it's worth saying a few words about business cards. Like them or loathe them, they are the 'currency' of most networking events. Asking for a business card signifies that you've enjoyed the conversation and would like to stay in touch. And even if that's a white lie, asking for a card as part of your 'leaving gambit' is both polite and positive. After all, if you don't get someone's card (or their contact details in some other guise), how are you going to stay in touch?

Certainly in most Western countries, the accepted norm is to ask for a card as you leave – and this serves the useful purpose of signifying, however subliminally, that the encounter is over. Only at business meetings (whether formal or informal), do you play the 'business card game' as people deal out cards to all their colleagues around the table. In many Eastern countries, in contrast, cards are exchanged at the start of any encounter, whether in a meeting room or at a less structured networking event.

Interestingly, business cards also embody other cultural values. In the East, they are treated formally, almost as if they are an extension of their owner's persona. They are given with both hands and received with both hands, and nobody in the East would dream of simply shoving someone's card in their pocket for future reference, as we in Europe and North America might well do. Perhaps here we 'Westerners' could learn from our colleagues in the East. Showing more respect for somebody's business card is, by implication, showing respect for them. And from personal experience, we can say that almost everybody responds positively to that.

The Devil's In The Detail

Next time you ask for, or are given, a business card, take the time to study it for a moment. Make a comment about some detail on the card – perhaps about the typography, the corporate logo, the colours or paper used. It doesn't have to be long or complicated: "That's a cheerful card, it certainly stands out from the pack" or "Very impressive – I like the embossed letters" will suffice.

Then watch for a pleased reaction from the card's owner. Although by no means obligatory, the fact that we have made the (admittedly small) effort to look at the card implies that we are also equally interested in its owner.

If you have a say in the matter (and not all of us do, of course), think long and hard about the design, the colours, and the format of your cards, as well as the actual words you use. Your business card can say as much about you as your clothes and behaviour do, so it's well worth paying attention to the detail. What impression do you want to create? Is the paper of the right quality? Could you use a different medium – such as plastic, a mini-CD or even a fridge magnet? Have you made good use of logos, images and colours? (Unfortunately, the image opposite isn't in colour or we would have included a very effective card for a company called Midas PR, who used gold lettering on a glossy black background.) What information or image should grace the front of the card? And what about the back? Is there too much information on the card, or not enough?

There is no simple right answer, of course. The sort of card that suits, say, a lawyer might be quite inappropriate for someone who lives in the world of PR and media. What is reliable for one is dull and boring to the other. Here are a few business cards that we've collected over the years. How would you describe them? In each case, we've given alternative adjectives – it all depends on your point of view.

- Dull and boring / reliable and consistent

- Creative and intriguing / unprofessional

- Corporate and dependable / bureaucratic and slow

- Entrepreneurial and flexible / unreliable.

Jenny Levin

Top Flat
45 Mowbray Road
London NW6 7QS

Cell: +44 (0)7944 781 369
Tel: +44 (0)20 8451 6816

e-mail: jenny_levin@yahoo.co.uk

iOpener

Jess Pryce-Jones

28 Warnborough Road
Oxford OX2 6JA UK
Tel   +44 (0)1865 511522
Fax   +44 (0)1865 552918
Mobile +44 (0)7967 010469
jess.prycejones@iopener.co.uk
www.iopener.co.uk

alison benson

indigo research
6B northway london nw11 6pa
tel: 020 8731 9977 fax: 020 8731 9229
e-mail: mail@indigoresearch.co.uk

bearhug

Paul Robison

Bearhug Ltd
Croftholme Studio
9 Albert Street
Cambridge
CB4 3BE
UK

tel/fax: +44 (0)1223 511955
mobile: +44 (0)7050 300977
e-mail: paul_r@bearhug.ltd.uk
www.bearhug.ltd.uk

JOHN SIMMONS

John Simmons
26 Grasmere Road
London N10 2DJ

Telephone 020 8245 0835
Mobile 'phone 07976 916502
Email johnsimmons@blueyonder.co.uk

ODGERS RAY & BERNDTSON

Sue Shipley
Partner

11 Hanover Square London W1S 1JJ
Tel: 020 7529 1111 Fax: 020 7529 1000
Direct line 020 7529 1099 Mobile: 07970 980137
sue.ship   @odgers.com

Bayer CropScience

B
A
Y
E
R

Smita Patel
C Chem. MRSC. MBA

Tel. + 49 69 305 - 839 61
Fax + 49 69 35 60 38
Smita.Patel@
bayercropscience.com

Jane James

Neale Phillips

Head of Insurance
British Gas Business
Millstream West, Maidenhead Road,
Windsor SL4 5GD

(M) 07769 547036
(E) neale.phillips@centrica.com

www.britishgasbusiness.co.uk

Some people we've met take this notion even further. Keith, an independent consultant who participated in one of our public workshops, told us that he had no less than three different cards.

A Card For Every Occasion

> 7 Woodhall Drive
> Pinner
> Middlesex
> HA5 4TG
>
> **KEITH KIKUCHI-ALLSOPP**
>
> tele: 020 8428 9706
> mob: 07913 487 534
> email: kkallsopp@btinternet.com

One of Keith's business cards just bears his name, address and contact details. To quote Keith: "If I'm going to an interview or meeting someone whom I already know, then they're generally already aware of my qualifications and (especially if I am better qualified than they) may feel I am trying to appear superior... People often feel very uncomfortable employing someone better qualified than they are."

> **KEITH KIKUCHI-ALLSOPP MBA, MCMI**
>
> 7 Woodhall Drive
> Pinner
> Middlesex
> HA5 4TG
>
> tele: 020 8428 9706
> mob: 07913 487 534
> email: kkallsopp@btinternet.com

Another card has, in addition, 'letters' after his name. Keith says: "Conversely, if I am networking and I want to get the message across that I am a senior or experienced manager with a sound academic background, the letters on this card allow me to concentrate on my specialisms and areas of specific interest."

> **KEITH KIKUCHI-ALLSOPP MBA, MCMI**
>
> 7 Woodhall Drive   International
> Pinner   Telecommunications
> Middlesex   Specialist
> HA5 4TG
>
> tele: 020 8428 9706
> mob: 07913 487 534
> email: kkallsopp@btinternet.com

The third card, which Keith rarely uses now, includes the designation 'International Telecommunications Specialist'. "I used to use this card when I was talking to telecoms people, but I've stopped using it now as I am trying to move sideways."

The truth is that the proliferation of high-quality and affordable printers means that it's easy to tailor your business card to suit the situation. So do remember that business cards play several roles: they 'say something' about us and the organisation to which we belong, and they make it easy to exchange contact details. After all, most of us find it hard enough to remember people's names, let alone their email addresses or phone numbers. Which leads us neatly on to our next subject – names, and how to remember them.

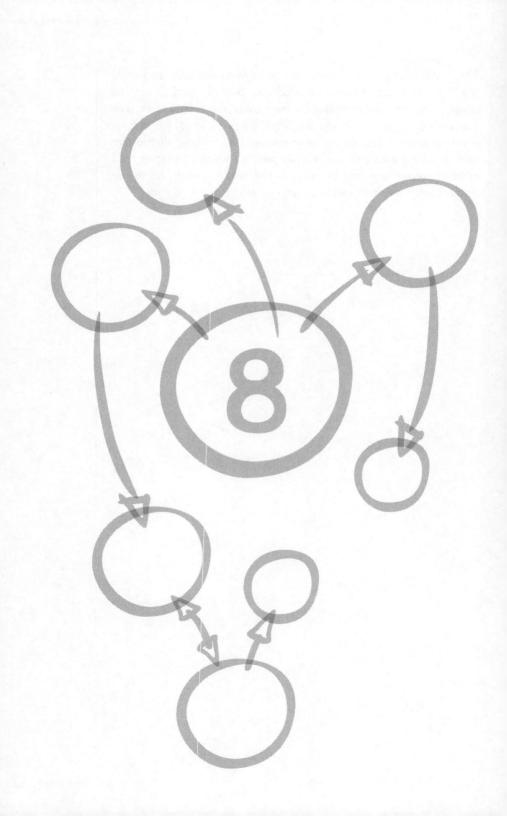

CHAPTER EIGHT

What's in a Name?

A person's name is his most prized
possession, and there is nothing more
pleasing to him than hearing his own
name or having it remembered by others.

HARRY LORAYNE (memory feat performer and author)

t's been said that one of the biggest compliments you can pay someone is to be able to recall their name instantly days, weeks, months or even years after one short meeting. Equally, forgetting a name or hailing someone by the wrong name may not spell disaster but it invariably gets an encounter off on the wrong foot. Such blunders are often laughed off, but the subconscious message that such an error sends out is "You are not important/memorable enough for it to be worth remembering who you are."

What The Papers Say

Tony's mother was visiting an old friend in Primrose Hill, an area of London in which she had brought up the family, but from which she had moved away many years previously. She needed some stamps, so popped into the local newsagent – a shop she hadn't been into for at least ten years. The proprietor, on seeing her, greeted her with the words "Mrs Newton, how nice to see you again! How have you been?"

Tony's mother, who is herself one of those people who remembers names and faces, and makes friends very easily, was hugely impressed and thoroughly flattered by the experience.

This episode set us wondering about the dynamics of this interaction. Did the newsagent remember Mrs Newton simply because he had an exceptional memory for names – or had there been something about her demeanour all those years ago, or something very specific that she had done, that made him able to retrieve her name, seemingly effortlessly? Either way, she had obviously somehow impressed him, and he certainly impressed her. The central questions from a networking perspective become:

■ What can you do to ensure that you impress others by being demonstrably able to remember their name?
■ What can you do to help the people you meet to remember *your* name?

How can you expect people to retain a strong mental image of you, or keep you 'front of mind' for a business (or other) opportunity if they can't even remember your name?

If you need convincing that names are very special, here's a real life situation to prove the point.

CASE STUDY

Judith Is Surprised

I was sitting quietly in an airport lounge, fully engaged with my laptop, working on an important presentation. Every so often I glanced at my watch to check the time, because I knew with total certainty that I was so engrossed in my work that I wouldn't hear my flight being called.

Suddenly I sat bolt upright, and looked around worriedly. For a few seconds, I had no idea what had disturbed my concentration. Then I heard my name being called on the loudspeaker. Astonished and rather bemused, I approached the information desk to find out what was happening. I had only heard my name – the rest of the message was in a foreign language!

Proof, we suggest, that your name really is one of your prized possessions. As the next case study shows, however, knowing someone's name can be pivotal to making something happen, as people respond to their name in a quite remarkable fashion when a job title is all too easy to ignore.

Judith Learns A *Very* Painful Lesson – Part 1

I'd cycled in London for years, with no mishaps. Then one day an inattentive driver opened the door of his parked car in my face. The end result: a stay in hospital to mend several broken ribs.

Early on, I feebly asked: "Nurse, can you help me please?" The response: zero. So I tried again, summoning all my strength and trying to sound at least slightly commanding (difficult when you're tired, drugged up and traumatised). Still nothing.

Just then, another nurse came in, whose name I'd got during a previous shift and could remember because I had a friend with the same name. The association I'd made was one of opposites. My friend was blonde, plump and white, while her namesake nurse was from Kenya: tall, elegant and black. So without thinking, I said, "Lucy, can you help me to sit up a bit straighter?" Bingo! Lucy turned round, smiled and quickly sorted me out.

Later that same day, I repeated the experiment, with identical results. No name: no response. Not out of malice, but because they either didn't hear me at all or had too much to do and assumed that someone else would help.

If we're agreed on the importance of names, let's start with the business of remembering other people's. Imagine the following scenario: you're talking to a group of people, at a social gathering or a networking event, and you strike up a conversation with someone you've never met before, having made the usual mutual introductions. A few minutes later, a colleague of yours comes up to you, naturally expecting to be introduced to your new acquaintance and you realise with horror that you've completely forgotten the name of the person you've been chatting to so animatedly!

Recognise the scene? You'd be unusual if you didn't because, when we ask that question in our workshops, almost invariably every hand in the room goes up – so the good news, as so often, is that you're not alone.

There's no single infallible answer to this problem, but there are several tricks and techniques that can help avoid or alleviate potential embarrassment. Try them out and see which works best for you – people's memories work in different ways, and what may be a godsend for you may be useless to me. But first it's crucial to understand the fact that 'hearing' and 'listening' are not synonymous. Many people claim that they have a poor memory for names, but isn't it funny how that memory problem can be so selective?

DO TRY THIS

White Noise

Turn your radio on, leaving it tuned to whatever station it was on previously. Make yourself a cup of tea or coffee, then settle down to read the following excerpt from "Estimating the Ripple Effect of a Disaster" (to which we referred in Chapter 2) as carefully as you can before answering the questions about it that you'll find on page 151. Don't even look at the questions until you've read and fully digested the excerpt.

> With appropriate caution, we can use the network scale-up model to answer the reporter's questions: How many people would be one or two links away from people who did or could have experienced the attacks on September 11, 2001? Assuming that 50,000 people could have experienced the attacks at the World Trade Center or the Pentagon or on the hijacked planes that day; that 20,000 actually had experienced the attacks; that about 6,333 are currently missing and presumed to have died; and assuming t is about 250 million, m would be, respectively, about 0.058, 0.023, or 0.0073, to two significant figures. (We'll quote estimates from here on out to two significant figures.)
>
> That is, across the U.S., each person knows, respectively, about 0.058, 0.023 or 0.0073 of a person who experienced, in one way or another, the calamity of

continued overleaf

continued from previous page

September 11th. (We use t = 250 million because that was the approximate population of the U.S. when we developed and tested the model and obtained the figure of c = 290.) We expect the distribution of answers across the U.S. to the question "How many do you know who experienced the attack on the WTC or the Pentagon on September 11th?" to consist largely of 1s and 0s, so we might treat the above m values as proportions, in which case about one person in 17, 43, or 140, respectively, knows someone who experienced the attack in one way or another.

We know, however, that if someone knows someone in a population they will tend to know others in the population, and this will almost certainly be true for those living in the New York City and Washington, D.C. metropolitan areas. We represent this by a "lead-in" factor, 8, which is the average number of members of a population known by those who know at least one member of the population. In general 8 > 1.0, so including this factor in our calculations should improve our estimates of m.

In previous work (Johnsen et al. 1995), based on General Social Survey data, we obtained lead-in factors for the populations of homicides, suicides, and AIDS victims of about 1.60, 1.26, and 1.75, respectively. The relatively low figure for suicides points to the relative social isolation and stigmatization of those who commit suicide, while the relatively high figure for AIDS reflects the relatively high social cohesiveness of those afflicted with AIDS despite stigmatization. We think that the figure for homicides reflects the fact that this is a population that is neither stigmatized nor uninteresting and that is generally not a cohesive group (though their survivors might be). We think that people who experienced the attack of September 11 are in this category, so we assume a lead-in factor of 1.60 for these populations.[1]

1. H. Russell Bernard et al, "Estimating the Ripple Effect of a Disaster", *Connections*, Vol. 24, No. 2, 2001, pp. 19-20.

The questions:

1. If the radio was tuned to a talk station, what was being said?
2. If the radio was tuned to a music station, what was playing?

Could you answer our questions? We'd be surprised if you could! The fact is that human beings aren't very good at multi-tasking. When we meet someone for the first time, most of us, being visual creatures, are focusing more on what we see than what we hear, with the consequence that the name, when it's given, often goes straight over our head. Ultimately, it's not really a memory problem, it's just that we never really listened in the first place.

Here's a step-by-step approach that should help deal with the problem.

1. Make sure that when someone introduces themselves (or is introduced to you), you actually listen to the name. If the name isn't clear (mumbled, unclear against background noise, foreign or just plain unusual), ask for it again immediately and if necessary ask for it to be spelled so you can 'see' it in your mind's eye. Don't let yourself get cornered into that uncomfortable position of having to ask for somebody's name again after you've been speaking to them for twenty minutes. But if you do find yourself there, just remember that you wouldn't be insulted if someone said to you "I'm really sorry, I'm useless at names, and I've just realised that I've forgotten yours!"

2. Is there anything in their name that is worthy of comment? If one of the reasons that we don't remember names is that we don't find the information important or interesting enough to engage us, then we have to fool the brain into thinking that the information is important. So...

■ **If you know someone else with the same name, mention it or at least bring that person to mind to create a mental association**

■ **If the name relates to a place, picture that person in that place**

■ **If the name conjures up a mental picture or even a 'sounds like' association, hang the name on that peg.**

Do bear in mind the advice of memory expert Harry Lorayne that one of the keys to success is to make the mental association as ludicrous as possible: it seems our brains are wired to respond better that way – think about your own weird dreams and you'll agree that it's true!

CASE STUDY

Hooked By Tony

While on holiday in Antigua, we met a couple by the pool whose names were Mike and Anne. Common names perhaps, but in some ways more difficult to remember because of that. So I made the mental association with an estate agent named Mike Anton, through whom we were in the process of buying a house: the ludicrous picture of these two people sitting in a Northumberland estate agent's office in their bathing costumes gave me the association 'Mike Anne-ton', which is now lodged firmly (and probably permanently) in my head.

To try to give a flavour of the power of such visual associations, let's turn the process on its head and present you with a couple of mad 'mental images' and see if you can follow the thought process that has led to that image.

You're terrible at remembering people's names, but now imagine that the chap you've just met and are chatting to at a reception is standing at the top of Nelson's column in London's Trafalgar Square wearing an admiral's hat, waving a gas bill and shouting down at you "How much???"

Could his name perhaps be Bill Nelson?

We've deliberately used Nelson in order to make the point that these things are highly personal – anyone not versed in British history couldn't have chosen this mental image in the first place.

And how about this one? The person you're now sitting across the desk from has told you his name, but not given you a business card. You didn't have a pen handy to jot his name down and you're concerned that you'll forget it and embarrass yourself. So you picture him standing at the top of a huge vertical drop with a flight of old-fashioned plaster ducks flying over his head.

This one reminds us that our brains actually like a good pun; the more groan-worthy and outlandish the better, just like our dreams. Add to that some weird visual imagery – note that we're imagining a flight of plaster ducks from a 1950s British living room wall, not boring real ducks – so here you have a man on a cliff with ducks on... cliff ducks on... Cliff Dixon.

Of course, not all names lend themselves to the technique, but it's amazing how many names can be broken down into component parts that will at least give you a fighting chance of making a memorable association. If you doubt that these tools are powerful for those occasions when it's imperative that you absolutely 'nail' someone's name, see if you can now get those Bill Nelson and Cliff Dixon mental pictures out of your head! Chances are they'll be there for a good while to come whether you like it or not.

Before we move on to the next tip, here's a word of caution. If you're going to make an association, make sure you get it right!

Judith Learns A *Very* Painful Lesson – Part 2

I was recovering from a cycling accident. Having learnt that names mattered, I made a special effort to remember my doctors' names.

One of the consultants looking after me was called Mr Hayward. I immediately associated him with the Hayward Gallery on London's South Bank. "Easy," I thought, "there's nothing to this name association game!"

Imagine his surprise (and my embarrassment) when, on our next meeting, my mind dulled somewhat by my rather sorry medical state, I greeted him very positively with "How nice to see you, Mr Tate." I had got my art galleries mixed up, and doubtless Mr Hayward thought that more than my ribs were in need of repair.

3. Use it or lose it. When someone gives you their name, try and use it in the conversation. Not only does it help fix the name in your head, but calling someone by name can attract and renew their attention. Making a point of using their name when ending the conversation or saying goodbye also pays that person the ever important psychological compliment that says "You're important enough for me to retain your name for more than ten seconds." You might be surprised to find what a difference actually saying someone's name out loud makes but that leads us to another word of caution – use it in moderation.

CASE STUDY

Familiarity Breeds Contempt

John is a senior finance executive with a blue-chip company. During a coffee break at a conference, he struck up an interesting conversation with Antonio. Then, says John, Antonio's friend Geraldo joined them. Which is when things started to go downhill.

Geraldo turned out to be much less sophisticated, and pounced on John's first name: "A pleasure to meet you, John." ... "Oh, yes, John, that sounds fascinating." ... "I've always been especially interested in bond options, John, how lucky that it's your speciality." ... "John, let me tell you about my experience..." And so it went on. Geraldo's over-eager use of his name, and only his first name at that, irritated John. Once or twice would have been fine, but half a dozen times was definitely over the top!

John extracted himself pretty smartly from the conversation. Later in the afternoon, though, he sought out Antonio, gave him his business card and invited him to call. Antonio had impressed John with the fact that he had:

■ Listened rather than talked too much about himself

■ Seemed genuinely interested in the conversation

■ Restrained himself from uttering the killer phrase "I'm looking for a job"

■ Been able to introduce John by name (*and* used both his first name and surname – a mark of respect when talking to someone more senior than yourself) at the point at which Geraldo first joined the conversation.

4. If someone has an unusual or difficult name, ask them to spell it or write it down for you, as seeing something in black and white can often help you remember it. Either say quite simply, "I'll never remember that... let me write it down so I can look at it" or, alternatively, ask them for a business card, which kills two birds with one stone. If the spelling of the name doesn't seem to have much in common with its pronunciation, use your own version of phonetic spelling to jot down the name the way it sounds. You may think you'll remember it, but we know from long experience that you won't. The importance of this is that, as we've said before, people tend to be protective of their names. If you call them up subsequently and stumble over their name, the psychological message you're sending them – regardless of the verbal content – is "You told me your name but I didn't pay enough attention to get it right." Equally, making the effort to get a difficult name right is a great way to get someone on your side.

DO TRY THIS

Loud And Clear

Here's a selection of 'difficult' names that we've encountered over the years. Some are difficult because they're unusual; others are just plain awkward, however good your English. There's no reason why you should know how to pronounce them – which is why recording their phonetic pronunciation is so useful. It's just not worth trusting your all-too-fallible memory to get it right.

Maciej Jura	pronounced	Mach-ee-ay Yura
Eke	pronounced	Ee-kee
Braude	pronounced	Brow (as in 'brown')-dee
Booij	pronounced	Boy
Sprague	pronounced	Sprarg
Menzies	pronounced	Mingis

And finally, here's one that isn't difficult... just a very long tongue-twister from Sri Lanka that's quite easy if you just break it down into its component parts and take it slowly at first:

| Wikramanayake | pronounced | Wi-kra-ma-nay-a-ka |

Say the phonetic spellings to yourself until you feel you've got them fixed. Happy? Now go through the list again, saying them out loud. Did they come out right first time or did you stumble?

5. If you're in a knot of people in which the conversation ebbs and flows between participants, you could use a lull in which someone else in the group is being animated to surreptitiously jot down one or more of the names on the back of a business card. This does two things. First, as exam revision experts will tell you, writing something down engages a different part of the brain to simply reading or hearing it and helps to get it into your memory. Second, it provides an 'aide-memoire' that you can refer to later in the conversation (or the evening) under the pretence of idly flicking through a bunch of innocuous-looking business cards while the conversational ball is in someone else's court – with the caveat that you mustn't make it look as if you've suddenly stopped paying attention to a conversation that's directed at you!

DO TRY THIS

Testing, Testing

While we can offer hints and tips, anyone who says "I can't remember names" and genuinely wants to work at improving their memory for names, faces, lists or just about anything else should get hold of the book *How to Develop a Super Power Memory* by Harry Lorayne, who's quoted at the head of this chapter. At the very least, it's worth taking a look at www.harrylorayne.com because the ideas he promotes really do work if (and here's the caveat) you're prepared to put in the spadework.

IN A NUTSHELL

People's memories function in different ways, so you need to find the trick for remembering names that works best for *you*.

Remembering names in the longer term presents a rather different problem: the information isn't deemed important enough to remember; it isn't called to mind frequently enough to keep it fresh;

and, perhaps most important, we don't have any long-term mental 'peg' on which to hang that particular piece of information.

So how can we improve the situation? A good place to start is to recognise that our brains do need the occasional refreshing of data. We've experienced and heard of numerous occasions when a quick flick through the contact database before a meeting or event not only helps with the names of people who are likely to be present but also refreshes the brain as to the personal information about them that we know is crucial to paying them the compliment that they are important.

Once you've checked out the names of the people you will, or might, be meeting, don't forget to remind yourself how to pronounce that name. And remember, what you say silently in your head can be very different from what comes out of your mouth...

CASE STUDY

Tony Nearly Trips Up

I was on my way down to the West Country to interview Dr Zbikowski. I was looking forward to hearing about his work, and considered myself pretty well prepared for the meeting. Having travelled to Poland several times, I thought I had got used to the unsettling spelling of Polish names. Even so, I practised the name 'Zbikowski' over and over in my head so as to be able to pronounce it fluently and nonchalantly at the reception desk.

On arrival, I strode confidently to the receptionist. "Hello, my name's Tony, Tony Newton. I'm here to see Dr Zbi... Zbiv... Zbikow." The result? A smirking receptionist and a firm resolution to practise all difficult names out loud in future.

Directed by the receptionist across the deserted campus to Dr Zbikowski's office, I took the opportunity to articulate his name to cars, lamp posts, trees and a dog, such that by the time I came to knock on my interviewee's door, I could smile confidently and say "Dr Zbikowski? Hello, I'm Tony, Tony Newton", without the hint of a tongue twist.

The fact is that saying something out loud requires very different coordination, musculature and articulation than simply thinking it or saying it under your breath.

Of course, all this can be turned on its head. From a networking perspective, you clearly want people to remember who you are so that there's no embarrassing silence on the other end of the phone when you call and they struggle to remember who on earth you are. So why should it be any different if the tables are turned, and how do you get people to remember *your* name? We covered the importance of name badges in an earlier chapter and it's worth re-iterating that, if name badges aren't provided at an event, there's nothing to stop you making or improvising your own.

There's also a neat little ploy we'd like to share with you:

DO TRY THIS

You Only Give Twice

We've all heard the immortal lines "The name's Bond, James Bond" and, while we're certainly not suggesting that you attend your next networking event in a white dinner jacket, there's an interesting trick to be learned here.

If you go up to someone and say "Hello, my name's John Smith", the chances are that your name will go in one ear and straight out the other. And they'll probably be too embarrassed to ask you to repeat it. But if you change the semantics slightly and say "Hello, I'm John... John Smith", what you're effectively doing is saying "I'm giving you my name, but you might not be paying attention, so I'm going to give you another chance to catch it."

Try it. It really does work.

Building on that theme, we'd like to remind you of the obvious: your name is very familiar to you. You've had it for many years, after all. But to anyone you meet for the first time, it's completely new. So you need to combat your nerves and perhaps a noisy environment to make absolutely sure that you don't mumble, rush or whisper, and that you give your name slowly and clearly. And if you aren't speaking your mother tongue (or you have a strong accent), practice on a few friendly ears to make sure that what you say can be interpreted correctly by the average native speaker.

IN A NUTSHELL

Your name is very familiar, and important, to you – but it isn't to others. So helping them to remember your name is useful to you as well as to them.

If you yourself have a name that other people always seem to have difficulty with, it's even more important to make sure that your listener picks it up correctly. It's hard enough grasping and remembering a familiar sort of name in the stress of a first meeting or the noise of a cocktail party; it's ten times more difficult if the actual name itself adds to the pressure.

So what else can you do to improve the situation? There are various 'coping mechanisms' that we've seen people use. Having your business card ready when giving your name can help: if your listener seems to be having difficulties, point out your name on your business card to turn it into a positive conversational point rather than a problem. An added benefit is that it gets your business card into their hands without them asking or you offering!

Another idea, and this doesn't apply only to people with 'difficult' names, is to offer a ready-made association of your own. That way, the person you're speaking to is spared the embarrassment of having to say, "Sorry, I didn't catch your name."

An Amazon In Disguise?

The scene: morning coffee prior to the start of a workshop. As we stand around chatting and finding out about the participants, a petite woman joins the group.

We introduce ourselves, and so does she. "My name's Aquila, and I'm from the Philippines", she says in a very soft voice that matches her stature. "But no one in England seems to be able to remember my name, when I tell them the first time, so now I say it's Aquila... like A KILLER!" And as she says this, her voice rises and she accompanies the outburst with a downward stabbing motion that would have got her a part in a remake of *Psycho*.

Aquila was right, of course. Neither of us have ever forgotten her... She was also pretty brave, choosing that association. It's certainly worth thinking about the impression you want to create when offering your association, as our next example shows.

Judith Meets Hans Christian Or Pamela?

At a workshop at London Business School, an MBA student cheerfully told me: "I tell them my name is James Anderson, like Pamela!"

Being at least 20 years older than him, with a liberal smattering of grey hair, I was forced to ask: "Who's she?" Amid general laughter and disbelief, I was told exactly who she was! As I blushed wildly, I desperately sought a way of extracting a valid teaching point from all this.

"There is a serious point here," I said. "Aside from me feeling uncomfortable that I don't know who Pamela Anderson is, you

continued overleaf

continued from previous page

need to think hard about the image you want to create. Hans Christian Andersen just might be a more appropriate association in certain circumstances."

or

For good luck, here's a third example that demonstrates great forethought and imagination.

CASE STUDY

Tony Gets Three In One

I was calling a new client to finalise the arrangements for a workshop. My problem, though, was that I'd been sent a direct telephone number and the name of Jane McAnerney, the administrator in charge, by email. I had no idea on which of the four syllables of her last name the emphasis should fall. There was no one to whom I could turn for advice, so the only thing to do was just pick up the phone.

"Hello, is that Jane?" I asked.

"Speaking," came the reply.

"Hi Jane, this is Tony Newton calling about the workshop. Just before we go any further, this is slightly embarrassing, but can you put me straight about how to pronounce your surname so I don't get it wrong?"

"No problem. Everyone has trouble with it and I'm used to hearing just about every pronunciation there is. The secret is just to remember that there are three of us here."

I thought I must have misheard. "Three of you...?"

"Yes, Jane, Mack and Ernie – Jane McAnerney!"

Very clever, highly memorable and a great 'coping mechanism' to deal with a persistent problem.

As we'll say several times in this book, networking is a two-way street. So helping others to remember your name really is the mark of a competent and conscientious networker – and, of course, it might also benefit you.

DO TRY THIS

Remember Me

Finally, as we close the chapter on names, think about your own first and last names. What association could you offer to help people remember you and your name for a long time to come?

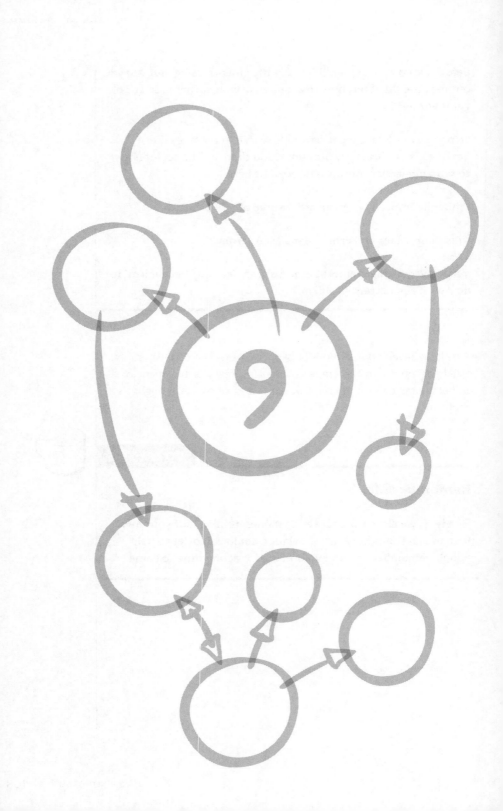

CHAPTER NINE

But I Don't Know Anyone!

A desk is a dangerous place from which to watch the world.

JOHN LE CARRÉ *The Honourable Schoolboy*

One of the most frequent comments we hear when working with people who have made, or are planning to make, a major change in their career path or geographic location is that they don't know many people or have a very small network. We believe that this isn't true, and this chapter is all about helping you think broadly, creatively and actively about how to widen your circle of acquaintances. As you expand and activate your network, we hope you'll quickly come to recognise just what a unique asset you have.

Implicit in the complaint are two clues which hint at the mindset of the complainant:

1. They expect new contacts to somehow parachute into their lives with little active effort from themselves. The world just doesn't work like that.

2. They are (probably) mentally discounting many real and potential contacts and sources of referral that don't spring readily to mind.

We talked many pages ago about how small a world we live in, and the things we can do to put ourselves in the path of good information and opportunities. But sometimes we need a kick start or a helping hand and, as both of this book's authors have made career and geographic changes, that's something we can talk knowledgeably about.

Let's start with a success story.

CASE STUDY

Barbara Gets Out And About

"I came to London from East Anglia, where I had lived all my life. I didn't know a soul – well, only two people, to be absolutely honest. Goodness only knows how I thought I was going to manage – especially as my profession was working as a freelance IT consultant. If that doesn't demand a wide network of contacts, I don't know what does!

"I floundered for a bit, getting nowhere fast. Then I got a newsletter from my professional organisation and noticed that my local branch was having a speaker. I went along, got chatting to some people – and during the evening something someone said sparked off a bright idea.

"Next day I called the branch secretary and asked if there was any way I could help out. She nearly bit my hand off, so to speak. Before I knew it, I had been co-opted onto the main committee, and found myself in the thick of things – enjoying myself enormously and, more importantly, meeting lots and lots of people through whom I gradually established my professional reputation.

"Now, three years later, I have more work than I can handle *plus* a network of contacts that I can call on if:

1. I find myself short of work.

2. I need any advice, or help."

What Barbara has done here is to make herself both active and visible, and it's worth highlighting the importance of these two behaviours and the distinction between them.

Clearly, joining an organisation is a useful and obvious step in creating a network in a new environment – so obvious that we almost hesitate to mention it, but we're often amazed at how little people sometimes do to help themselves in this respect. But those organisations are not necessarily the most obvious ones and, if you've taken on board the ideas we've already set out in this book, then you'll know that your next job could come about as a result of a conversation with someone in your creative writing group, or that your next romance could be the result of a chance encounter at the Institute of Actuaries.

When we probe deeper, we discover that most people never stop to question the basic mechanisms of how we make acquaintances, and how some of those acquaintances become friends. There's a wealth of academic literature about how friendships develop, and the two lessons that stand out are that:

1. People seem to make friends more on the basis of shared behaviours and activities than shared attitudes

2. The greater the mutual visibility and exposure (i.e. shared experience), the greater the likelihood that friendship will result.

Which can be distilled into a third lesson:

3. Getting to know people can actually be quite hard work, requiring a significant input of time and effort.

IN A NUTSHELL

Extending your network takes effort. It won't happen by itself.

This is where so many people fall down, expecting the effort that they need to put into making new acquaintances as an adult to be no different from that required as a child.

As we grow up, most of us develop friends out of the multitude of acquaintances who surround us in school, at university, through our job or through our leisure or domestic interests, but when suddenly thrust into a new environment, we conveniently forget that it was these institutions that were the wellspring of our network. So, in a new environment, we have to deliberately set out to find some new organisations to belong to. And we're not just talking here about being in a new job or a new location; it's just as relevant to finding yourself in a new cultural environment, such as when divorced or widowed.

Of course, not all new acquaintances will become friends, but remember that, from a networking perspective, acquaintances (those 'weak ties' we talked about in Chapter 2) are also important.

After a presentation on the power of networking to the Shell Women's Network, Cathy emailed us with a very personal and powerful story.

CASE STUDY

Networking Wisdom

"I've always been aware of the power of networking and I'm lucky enough to have built up a large network of friends and acquaintances who can give me support or impart knowledge on most subjects I'm likely to come across. In my last job I was known as the 'Fount of all Knowledge' because if I didn't know the answer I almost always knew someone who did.

"My mother and her sister both lost their husbands within two months of each other a couple of years ago. My mother has always been a very independent person and has a wide social network of friends and neighbours who, since my father's death, have been round to see her regularly, and take her out to pub quizzes, chapel lunches and coffee mornings or just to the shops. Her sister, my aunt, always relied heavily on her husband and *his* family and friends. Since he's been gone she's hardly left the house, has slumped into depression and has been in and out of hospital for various reasons. My mother is three years older than her sister, but is much fitter and happier, which I believe is purely due to the fact that she has the support of many different people around her, who can help out in many different ways. It gives her the confidence to face life each day on her own."

Cathy's story clearly shows how important it is to build that network of support before you find yourself in a new, and potentially difficult, situation – whether personal or professional.

Here's another case study that shows how a personal connection can yield something that is valuable to you but, often, pretty easy for them to provide.

Walking The Dog

Sandra took the trouble to get in touch again, some weeks after she had attended a presentation we had made.

"I came away from the session really invigorated, and enthused about the power of networking. But, as so often happens, the pressures of life took over and my good intentions remained just that: good intentions.

"Then my son, who is very keen on drama, decided that he was absolutely, definitely going to get to the Edinburgh Festival this year. But with very limited funds, he had no idea how he was going to afford the costs of travel, accommodation, tickets etc. Could I help?

"For some reason, the phrase 'the strength of weak ties' that you had emphasised at your networking session popped into my mind – and I decided to put it to the test. So I asked all sorts of people if they could possibly help out, since I thought that someone in my network just might know someone willing to lend my son a floor to sleep on for a few days.

"Guess what – a member of my dog-walking group came up trumps, and a friend of theirs offered my son a bed for the festival. Now I'm a believer – networking really does work."

IN A NUTSHELL

I'll get by with a little help from my friends.

So spreading a wide net is important, and that means thinking creatively about the sort of organisations you might want to belong to. For every one of us, our life can be illustrated by a Venn diagram that encapsulates the reality of our daily lives.

For a well-balanced individual, that diagram might look something like this:

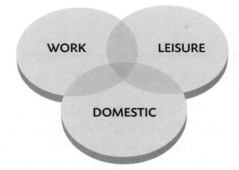

For the workaholic, like this:

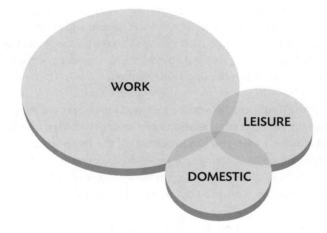

And for the busy housewife (or husband), like this:

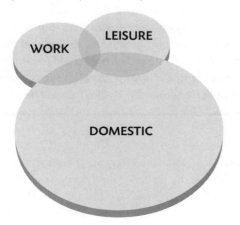

It's only when you dispassionately analyse your own situation that you start to see the gaps.

You Have To Be In It To Win It

What we're inviting you to do is to analyse your membership of organisations in terms of the three major areas that make up your life: work, leisure and domestic. By 'organisation', we mean any vehicle through which people can come together in a community.

Grab a sheet of paper and set out three headings: work, leisure and domestic. Under each heading, list the formal and informal groups you currently belong to. If you really have just moved into a new career, location or cultural environment, chances are that at least one of those lists is looking rather empty.

So draw a line under the list you've just made and start thinking instead about all those organisations you *could* get involved with. This probably isn't a list you can jot down off the top of your head, and the more research you have to do to compile this list, the more useful it's likely to be to you because it means that you're thinking about opening up previously unexplored channels.

For example, you might be spurred to find out whether your industry or professional association has a branch structure that you could join. On the leisure front, you might suddenly remember that you used to enjoy choral singing, tap dancing or scuba diving, and be encouraged to search for local clubs offering these activities. On the domestic front, could joining a residents' association, special interest group, expat group or even political party help you get networked with like-minded people?

To deal head on with the comment (which we know will be forthcoming from some readers) "But I don't have time for this stuff!", our answer must be "Do you have the time NOT to do this stuff?" Without repeating here all the reasons why you should network that we outlined earlier, the simple fact is that, if you feel that you are not well connected for whatever reason, then it is you, and you only, who can change your situation.

Sometimes, of course, you might attend a meeting and come away with nothing at all. Other times, you'll meet lots of interesting and potentially helpful people. You never can tell in advance – and, as they say, nothing ventured, nothing gained.

But just in case you have any lingering doubts about the usefulness of all this, here's a case study sent to us by Neil, a budding entrepreneur who came to a workshop we ran at Leeds University Business School.

CASE STUDY

Neil Reaps Rewards

"I went to an evening 'do' straight after the training. It went well. In the three hours after we finished:

■ I drank a couple of free beers and ate some pizza!!!!

■ Met some undergraduates in sports science who want to set up an outdoor activity centre.

■ Met a guy from Leeds Metropolitan University who runs lots of start-up business support functions and workshops – contacts galore I'm sure.

■ Met the new guy at Leeds Uni who is supporting business start-ups in conjunction with three other regional universities – good for intellectual property advice.

■ Found out about an incubator cell – 18 free desks for one year for new businesses – sponsored by the Uni.

■ Found out about small-scale VC funding up to £250k through local enterprise funding.

continued overleaf

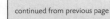

continued from previous page

■ I learned that I can submit a business plan I'm doing at Leeds to a competition for £10k. Win or lose I get support to implement it.

■ Met and swapped cards/email with the MD of a new company and first to use incubator facility. I've followed up today – gave him details of the guy who is designing my company logo.

■ Met a young guy who is trying to get into sports journalism. I know a guy who writes footy reports for the *Guardian* – his dad runs a manufacturing company up the road from where my old factory premises were in Manchester. Seems like a fair contact swap. I will meet him at the business school to sort it out.

"So, as you can see it was a successful evening. I tried the open stance next to the beers and was chatting to people before I knew it. Also saw some closed stances from established groups. Staying till the end also proved to be a good way to get hold of the organiser. Late night, but worth it.

"I'll continue to put the theory into practice and see what happens. As they say, the 'big man helps those who help themselves.'"

Everything we've discussed so far relates to making yourself visible but, as Barbara discovered in the case study that opened this chapter, that's only half the story. Being visible makes you a name on an address list and gets you the invitations, but if you really want to get the most from an organisation, you have to think about making yourself active within it, for a number of reasons:

1. The moment you make yourself active on the organisational or management side of things, other people need to know who you are, and the chances are that your name will start appearing in emails, newsletters and the like. People will, quite rightly, begin to think of you as someone 'in the know'.

2. By being involved in decision making, you will learn more about other people within that organisation, and what makes them tick.

3. By being perceived as part of the 'inner circle', you automatically boost your status and put yourself in the path of good things potentially happening to you.

4. Being actively involved in an organisation gives you a ready-made opening and implicit permission to approach new faces at events with nothing more than "Hi, my name's John Smith and I'm on the organising committee. How are you enjoying this evening?" An easy way to get well and truly launched into a conversation.

Let's just stress here that we're emphatically not suggesting that you should join committees left, right and centre just for the connections they might bring: you have to have a genuine interest in them and something useful to offer, and it's perhaps worth mentioning that your reputation can suffer if you volunteer your services but then fail to deliver anything useful.

IN A NUTSHELL

Raising your profile involves being active and visible.

Using organisations to build a network in a new environment is one effective strategy, but there is a second and in many ways more obvious one that somehow gets ignored, overlooked or undervalued: being prepared to involve the people you already know in one environment to help you migrate to another.

The reason this avenue is so neglected is twofold. The first is that there's a wealth of research evidence showing that many of us (men to a greater extent than women) think that asking for help is a sign of weakness and perceive it as giving away power or exhibiting vulnerability. But the reality of today's complex business environment is that only people trapped in dead-end jobs never find themselves facing a challenge, so the ability and preparedness to harness an effective 'can do' network is actually a huge 'plus'.

The second is to do with our fixation with the 'here and now', which can make us forget about the people we used to know and blinkers us to all those on the periphery of our network who might be able to help establish us in our new environment if only we are prepared to ask the right questions and tell them what we are trying to achieve.

DO TRY THIS

We all know far more people than we can keep in conscious memory, so it's a useful exercise to start prodding the far reaches of our history to help bring into focus those people – those 'weak ties' – whom we've pretty much forgotten about, but who could perhaps help us get where we want to go.

At the top of a sheet of paper, jot down as precisely as you can a new environment into which you want to network yourself. Try to be specific, because if you don't ask the right question, you probably won't get the right answer. When it comes to putting this into practice, remember that the more detail you can offer people about what you want, the more likely they are to be able to point you in a useful direction.

Now look in turn at each of the groups labelled in the 'aide-memoire' below and let your mind wander as freely as you can over each group before moving on to the next.

STEPPING STONES

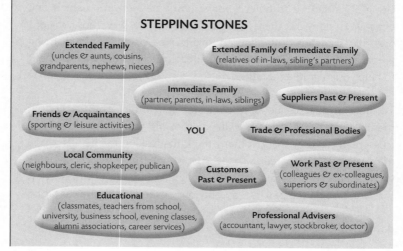

Try not to fall into the trap of thinking "They wouldn't remember me after all this time" or "Why would they bother to help me out?" We'll deal with that side of things in the next chapter.

Remember too that we're not looking for people whom you *know* have a connection that might help: if you already knew that, you've probably already brought that connection into play (and if you haven't, why haven't you?). The point is that, at this stage of the game, you don't know what contacts the people you know actually have, and the first step is to make sure that you are thinking as widely and creatively as possible about who you do actually know.

For the purposes of this exercise, focus on jotting down the names of people whom you have good reason to think might have one or more connections that could help you out. Surprised at some of the ghosts that have appeared from your past in each group? The human brain being what it is, you'll probably find more names and faces coming to mind quite unbidden over the next few days, now that we've got you thinking about them: if your subconscious is working overtime on your behalf, it's worth listening to what it has to say!

IN A NUTSHELL

You know far more people than you think you do.

Visualise your network as an iceberg. There's a small core (visible above the water) that is close and active. They're your friends, and the acquaintances with whom you maintain quite regular contact. When you're stuck for help or advice, they're the people who spring fairly readily to mind.

Hidden below the surface, though, are the many people who have slipped from your conscious memory. In the case of your friends' friends (and acquaintances), these are also the people who you don't know are in their network. If writing down the names of all the people you know you could ask for help is difficult, then when it comes to people two degrees of separation away from you, its pretty much impossible. You can really only make reasoned guesses: you know, maybe, that someone lived in Italy for a few years, so it's logical to surmise that they might be able to put you in touch with somebody who (for example) can help you make sense of the Italian tax system.

It's here that many of the social networking websites come into their own. As the opening quotation to this chapter stated, you just can't network from behind a desk. You do have to get out and about, and meet people. But what websites such as LinkedIn, Facebook and others can do is help make the networks of your friends and acquaintances more transparent to you. In the Italian example above, for instance, you could take a quick look at that particular friend's connections and see if there was somebody specific whom you'd like to ask for an introduction to.

If you think back to everything we said about the importance of weak ties, then it becomes obvious that the more people you can think of to rope in as your eyes and ears, and the more creative you can be about identifying those people, the more successful you are likely to be in your search.

But, given that we know just how difficult it can be to realise the true value of other people's networks, let's give you a real example of how this process actually helped someone.

CASE STUDY

Garth Finds An Unexpected Link

"Rob was a builder on a private estate near St Albans and has never worked in an office in his life. When we got together, we tended to talk about rugby, take a gun and go shooting rabbits. Despite our career differences (I was working in IT for a City law firm), we are both from New Zealand and got on really well together. About a year ago he moved back to New Zealand and I've not spoken to him since.

"My wife stayed in touch with Rob's wife, though, and they'd speak on the phone every so often. On one occasion, Rob answered and as they chatted my wife mentioned how, after my MBA studies, I was looking for different options and that finance particularly interested me.

"I'm sure Rob was primarily listening to my wife out of politeness. But when she mentioned my job hunt, he suddenly sparked up and said that he'd text Peter, the owner of the estate where he used to work in St Albans.

"It turns out that Peter is a vastly experienced banker and the founder and CEO of a leading financial data company – a fact that I think I had known, but simply forgotten. I gave Peter a call on his personal mobile and he was more than happy to meet with me following the text he had received from Rob giving him a heads-up that I would be making contact. We've had the meeting and it was extremely interesting and beneficial, with the end result that I'm hoping to do my MBA dissertation on one of their projects.

"If I do a good job, who knows where it may lead..."

In this example, neither Garth nor his wife had consciously thought about asking Rob for help. Yet Rob was able to refer Garth to an extremely helpful contact and, just by sending a single text message, potentially kick-started Garth's career change. Remember what Granovetter said in 'The Strength of Weak Ties' about "crucial information from people whose very existence they have forgotten"? Well, that's what this chapter has all been about – that's you!

Having a list of names from your past and from your wider network is one thing, but how to renew contact with them and enlist their help in building your brave new network? That's something we'll cover in the next couple of chapters.

CHAPTER TEN

Back at the Ranch

*Anyone can do any amount of work,
provided it isn't the work he is supposed
to be doing at that moment.*

ROBERT BENCHLEY *American columnist, author and humorist*

How many times have you heard a comment along these lines: "It was a great networking opportunity; a whole load of people took my business card, so it's bound to be productive!" Have you ever thought that yourself, then been surprised and mildly annoyed when not one of those people makes contact over the next few weeks? The fact is that, while the Bible tells us that it is better to give than to receive (and in most aspects of networking, we'd agree absolutely), with business cards, it's different.

As with so much in networking, the issue is one of retaining the initiative. If your focus is on getting your business card into someone else's hands, you're ceding control of the relationship to them: it's entirely up to them whether they call or email you... and that's assuming they don't mislay your card or dump it in the waste bin. Of course, we're not suggesting that you refuse to give cards to people who ask for them. What we are saying, though, is that, rather than push your card on to somebody, it's often more productive simply to ask for theirs. We've all been the victim of 'spray and pray' merchants who hand out their card to everybody in sight, thinking that they're 'networking'. Don't be one of them!

IN A NUTSHELL

It's often better to get a business card than to give one.

So you've been to a thoroughly enjoyable networking event, or just had an interesting conversation on a plane journey. Before you sign off for the day, you empty your pockets and/or bag of the business cards you've collected. What are you going to do with those cards that are now sitting on your desk or bedside table?

DO TRY THIS

Who On Earth Were They?

We're willing to bet that almost every reader of this book will have a small or large pile of business cards waiting for something to be done with them. Get that pile and take a look at every card. For each one, consider:

■ Did you follow up with that person in any way since they gave you their card?

■ Did you jot down anything on the card to remind you about that person, what you discussed or their interests? If not, what can you actually bring to mind about them? Anything at all?

■ Have you entered that person's details into any sort of database?

If the answer to the above is 'yes' on all three counts, you can probably skip the rest of this chapter; if not, please read on.

Why is it so important to follow up a meeting? The answer is absurdly simple: if you meet someone and don't follow up with them after the event, then you've had what is effectively a 'one night stand', which is unlikely to develop any further – until or unless you happen to meet them again. Only by following up within a sensible time frame after the event do you stand a reasonable chance of keeping your name 'front of mind' with your contact. If the follow-up is a good one, you have the added benefit of having raised your profile further, rather than having simply maintained it.

There is one particular type of follow-up that is worth mentioning in its own right, and that's the 'thank you' note. It's so easy to forget to say 'thank you', or not to bother or to leave it so long after the event that you think it's just too late. Here's a story that shows how failing to say 'thank you' can actually harm both your reputation and your financial wellbeing.

Nice Work If You Can Get It

Matthew told us about Neil, a friend of his who, having been made redundant, packed his bags and disappeared to the other side of the world for six months. On his return, Matthew and Neil met for dinner, and it was evident that Neil was looking for gainful employment at senior level, and for some consultancy work to keep him solvent until the dream job arrived.

Matthew's wife, Jane, who works in private equity, happened to be at an Investment Committee meeting a couple of days later, during which it was agreed that an external consultant would be needed to review some patents and licensing agreements. "That might be right up Neil's street, and he could certainly use the work," thought Jane and suggested that the executive working on the deal get Neil in for a chat.

Bear in mind that (a) Neil's ability to deliver was an unknown quantity to all concerned; (b) Jane had gone out on a limb in terms of her own credibility and reputation in recommending someone with no track record in private equity; and (c) this particular private equity group is one that most people would kill to work with.

After checking back via Matthew with Neil to confirm that he'd be interested in this work (and he was... very!), Jane gave the executive Neil's phone number and left them to it. Apart from Neil saying hello when he came into the office for his exploratory meeting, that was the last that either Jane or Matthew heard of the matter.

Some weeks later, Jane learned from the executive that Neil had indeed been engaged to do the required patent and license review, and that he'd carried out the work efficiently and to time. But did Jane or Matthew hear anything from Neil himself? Not a thing; not a 'thank you' card, call or email, let alone a bottle of wine for the several thousand pounds' worth of consultancy work that Jane had introduced him to.

> But now for the 'kicker': chatting to the same executive a couple of weeks later, Jane discovered that (to paraphrase) "You know, that chap Neil you recommended could have charged twice as much for what he did and we wouldn't have batted an eyelid."

If you were in Matthew and Jane's position, would you feel inclined to help Neil again? And do you think that either of them was going to contact Neil and tell him not to undercharge on his next contract with the firm? By not bothering to say 'thank you', Neil contrived simultaneously to undermine his own position and to lose out on some crucial information that might have significantly enhanced his own future earnings.

Here's another case study that illustrates how many people forget to say thank you, and how big an impression it can make.

CASE STUDY

An Apple A Day Keeps Judith Healthy

Early on in my career as an editor, I moved from a large to a small publishing house. The culture shock was pretty severe – from having only my small piece of the jigsaw to worry about, I found myself in charge of the entire publishing process.

What I knew about printing and production at that time could have been written on the back of the proverbial postage stamp. But I wasn't afraid of asking for help when I needed it and I was also particularly lucky to work with an experienced and understanding printer's rep. Herbert was a master of understatement – he guided me constantly with enormous tact.

At Christmas, Herbert's secretary contacted me asking me to choose a present. I'm an apple addict, so the thought of an entire box of Cox's Orange Pippins to eat my way through was bliss! As soon as the box arrived, I called Herbert to thank him. "Do you know, Judith," he said, "you're the only person who has ever,

continued overleaf

continued from previous page

in all my years in printing, bothered to say thank you. You can't imagine how good it makes me feel."

The simple fact that I had bothered to say thanks, like my mother taught me I should, cemented a working relationship that lasted for several years.

(As a postscript to this story, I haven't spoken to Herbert for over 25 years. While working on this book, I decided to try to renew contact. Luckily, Herbert has an unusual surname and there was only one phone book entry in his home town. I picked up the phone, and found myself telling a very surprised Herbert how much he had helped me at a difficult stage of my career. Thanks again, Herbert!)

A thank you, whether verbal or written, makes a huge impression, out of all proportion to the time and effort involved. Gratitude is one of those little things that make a big difference.

The change in mindset we're asking you to adopt is to realise that saying 'thanks' in particular and following up in general is not just to do with 'doing the right thing' but everything to do with healthy self-interest, because it makes the recipient feel good about themselves while at the same time enhancing your own profile and reputation. And it's not limited to saying 'thank you' for a crate of apples or a consultancy assignment.

IN A NUTSHELL

Saying 'thank you' isn't merely a question of politeness. It's also a question of enlightened self-interest.

Thank You Very Much

Before going any further, see if you can jot down ten valid reasons for saying 'thanks', and the effect you think that it might have on the recipient. It doesn't matter if some of your reasons seem flippant: the key point is that what you achieve by saying 'thanks' is actually an excuse to keep your name and profile uppermost in the mind of the recipient. When you've run out of ideas, compare your list with our suggestions below.

Ten reasons to say 'thanks':

1. Thanks for the book/theatre/restaurant/hotel recommendation

2. Thanks for the onward referral to a business contact

3. Thanks for the useful piece of business intelligence

4. Thanks for coffee/lunch

5. Thanks for the order

6. Thanks for the help

7. Thanks for a really stimulating conversation

8. Thanks for an excellent course/workshop/seminar/speech

9. Thanks for getting the job done well/on time/on budget

10. Thanks for taking the time to meet for a chat.

We know intellectually that following up is important, but the problem remains that research of our own shows that most of us still don't do it, as the following example demonstrates.

You Can Lead A Horse To Water...

Interim managers are a special breed, able to hit the ground running, working intensively on short-term assignments, often having to troubleshoot or manage sensitive projects.

Richard Lambert was for some time Chairman of the Interim Management Association, the professional body that represents the voice of the interim industry. He says: "Many senior managers who find themselves unwillingly jobless think that becoming an interim is an easy option, a way of earning a quick buck while looking for that perfect next job. We at the IMA wanted to dispel this illusion. Interims have to be exceptionally tough; it really isn't an easy option. So, we developed a one-day workshop which would give prospective interims a real insight into what they were letting themselves in for.

"The workshop is delivered by a third-party training company, but someone from the IMA always gives the introductory session. I remember one particular occasion. There were 15 attendees – and at the time I headed KPMG's interim practice. During the kick-off session, I stressed the importance of nurturing a strong network of contacts. Developing relationships, I said, was essential.

"How many of the 15 bothered to follow up with me, do you think? Just two – and of those, one was already working as an interim, and the other was clearly exceptionally bright! So despite my telling them to follow up (and don't forget, I was a pretty influential person in the industry), only two took my advice! It makes me want to weep!"

So what stops people from following up? We think that there are four key elements:

1. Not recognising the importance and value of the follow-up for staying 'front of mind' with the recipient

2. Not realising just how many things it is valid to follow up about

3. The almost universal (and almost universally bogus) complaint that "I'm too busy" or "I don't have time to do this stuff!"

4. Forgetfulness (which, it could be argued, is a variation of No. 1; after all, if something is important, you tend not to forget to do it).

IN A NUTSHELL

Follow up fairly quickly or you'll probably never get round to it.

Having accepted the premise that a timely follow-up is important, let's consider what constitutes a 'good' follow-up. Take a look at this email:

Hi,
Good to meet you last week. Just wanted to follow up and make sure you have my contact details.
Regards,

Sure, it's a follow-up, and it means that the sender can tick the mental box marked 'do follow-up', but what does it actually achieve? Does it make the recipient pleased to get it? Does it feel personal, or could the same email have been sent to pretty much anybody? Does it enhance the sender's credibility and reputation or undermine it? Does it do anything to jog the recipient's memory as to who the sender is and where or when they met? Does it pay the recipient any sort of psychological compliment?

Clearly not. So how do we improve matters? Here's an exercise that should help you find out and discover your own preferred style for following up. We can't engineer a meeting for you out of the pages of this book, but we can eavesdrop on one of the most famous meetings of all time.

Dr Livingstone I Presume?

What follows is an abridged extract from Henry Morton Stanley's own account of his meeting with Livingstone as published in his book *How I Found Livingstone*.

> We were now about three hundred yards from the village of Ujiji, and the crowds are dense about me. Suddenly I hear a voice on my right say, "Good morning, sir!"
>
> Startled at hearing this greeting in the midst of such a crowd of black people, I turn sharply around in search of the man, and see him at my side, with the blackest of faces, but animated and joyous – a man dressed in a long white shirt, with a turban of American sheeting around his woolly head, and I ask: "Who the mischief are you?"
>
> "I am Susi, the servant of Dr. Livingstone," said he, smiling, and showing a gleaming row of teeth.
>
> "What! Is Dr. Livingstone here?"
>
> "Sure, sure, Sir. Why, I leave him just now."
>
> In the meantime the head of the expedition had halted, and Selim said to me: "I see the Doctor, Sir. Oh, what an old man! He has got a white beard." My heart beats fast, but I must not let my face betray my emotions, lest it shall detract from the dignity of a white man appearing under such extraordinary circumstances.
>
> So I did that which I thought was most dignified. I pushed back the crowds, and, passing from the rear, walked down a living avenue of people until I came in front of the semicircle of Arabs, in the front of which stood "the white man with the gray beard."
>
> As I advanced slowly toward him I noticed he was pale,

looked wearied, had a gray beard, wore a bluish cap with a faded gold band round it, had on a red-sleeved waistcoat and a pair of gray tweed trousers. I would have run to him, only I was a coward in the presence of such a mob, – would have embraced him, but that I did not know how he would receive me; so I did what cowardice and false pride suggested was the best thing – walked deliberately to him, took off my hat, and said:
"Dr. Livingstone, I presume?"

"Yes," said he, with a kind, cordial smile, lifting his cap slightly.

I replaced my hat on my head, and he replaced his cap, and we both grasped hands. I then say aloud:

"I thank God, Doctor, I have been permitted to see you."

He answered, "I feel thankful that I am here to welcome you."

Then, oblivious of the crowds, oblivious of the men who shared with me my dangers, we – Livingstone and I – turn our faces towards his house. He pointed to the veranda or, rather, mud platform, under the broad overhanging eaves; he pointed to his own particular seat, which I saw his age and experience in Africa had suggested, namely,

continued overleaf

continued from previous page

a straw mat, with a goatskin over it, and another skin nailed against the wall to protect his back from contact with the cold mud. I protest against taking this seat, which so much more befitted him than me, but the Doctor would not yield: I must take it.

Conversation began. What about? I declare I have forgotten. Oh! we mutually asked questions of one another, such as:

"How did you come here?" and "Where have you been all this long time? – the world has believed you to be dead." Yes, that was the way it began: but whatever the Doctor informed me, and that which I communicated to him, I cannot correctly report, for I found myself gazing at him, conning the wonderful figure and face of the man at whose side I now sat in Central Africa.

The Doctor kept the letter-bag on his knee, then, presently opened it, looked at the letters contained there, and read one or two of his children's letters, his face in the meanwhile lighting up.

He asked me to tell him the news. "No, Doctor," said I, "read your letters first, which I am sure you must be impatient to read."

"Ah," said he, "I have waited years for letters, and I have been taught patience. I can surely afford to wait a few hours longer. No, tell me the general news: how is the world getting along?"

" Do you know that the Suez Canal is a fact – is opened, and a regular trade carried on between Europe and India through it?"

"I did not hear about the opening of it. Well, that is grand news! What else?"

■ ■ ■

> Imagine now that email existed in the late 1800s. Taking the part of Stanley, try using the preceding text and image to construct an email follow-up from yourself to Livingstone a few days after your historic meeting.
>
> We know it's tempting just to read straight on, but you'll get more out of the exercise if you pause here and take a few minutes to actually write something down. After all, that's what you'll have to do when writing a follow-up in the real world.

Now that you've got your historic email in front of you, let's see how it compares with our 'hit list'. We think that there are four strands to a good follow-up.

1. A 'hook'. Remind the recipient who you are and where you met: if they can't quite place you, the rest of the follow-up becomes pretty meaningless. In an era of spam, when the decision to read or delete an email is made in the blink of an eye, try to make sure that your subject line somehow shouts 'Read Me!'

People who come to our workshops often follow up afterwards. We can always tell who was awake during the workshop, and who was listening selectively, by what they write. Some launch straight in, without even a hint or reminder, sending us reaching for our own database to check the name against recent workshops. Others get as far as "We met on the workshop last Thursday". But those who were really paying attention manage to add something that, effectively, says "I'm the one who..." Almost invariably, that helps us place them (both literally and metaphorically) and makes us much more inclined to make the effort to stay in touch. Some of our favourite "I'm the one who..." lines include:

- **I'm the bald guy who was wearing strange shoes.**

- **I'm the tall, sad Frenchman.**

- **I'm the one in the red shirt who asked you all the awkward questions.**

- I'm the one who builds dry stone walls for a hobby.

- I'm the only Brazilian in my class.

2. Use what you learned from your meeting or the environment. If you can bring in something about your conversation or the recipient's interests, it shows that you not only took an interest in what they had to say but actually remembered it.

3. Say what you want (or what you have to offer). You can't assume that the recipient will remember a vague offer of help, advice or an onward referral made under the influence of alcohol or in a crowded, noisy room. And people can be surprisingly unimaginative when it comes to offering to put people in touch with each other, so if you think they know someone you'd like to meet, it probably won't do any harm to (gently and tactfully) make them aware of the fact. It may be, of course, that you don't actually want anything other than to stay in touch.

4. Tell them what's going to happen next. Will you call them? Can they expect something in the mail from you? If you're expecting the recipient to make the next move, tell them what that move is to avoid any uncomfortable misunderstanding.

These points don't all need to be woven into each and every email but, to mix a metaphor, the more buttons that you can press in each email the better.

If you can introduce a lightness of touch and perhaps a sparkle of humour into your follow-ups, it can make them that much more welcome and easier to read, and the best advice we can give for getting the 'tone of voice' right is to imagine that you're chatting with the recipient face to face rather than sitting at a keyboard or in front of a piece of notepaper.

DO TRY THIS

Dr Livingstone, Take Two

How would you rework your follow-up email in the light of the four strands we've now introduced? You may want to read the extract again and see just how much there is that might be worthy of comment. Remember that the point of the exercise is to use this dramatised encounter as a metaphor for the numerous meetings that you are likely to have in your professional and social life, and that the scenery and environment of your local conference venue can be every bit as useful to you as that of deepest Africa.

Clearly, there is no right and wrong answer here and one person's follow-up will differ markedly from the next. But here's our version, just to show that it is possible to hit all the targets in reasonably succinct but chatty style. What we've written may not exactly suit your own style, and of course we're having a bit of fun with it, but it's got to be better than "Hey Doc, Great to meet you. Stanley."

Dear Dr Livingstone,
It was an absolute pleasure to finally meet you last week in Ujiji, and to find you looking so content in your work when the outside world believed you to have succumbed to the perils of deepest Africa.
     I have to tell you now that, on first seeing you, having searched for so long, the temptation to run and embrace you was almost overwhelming. But my concern that this might not be perceived as a very 'English' way of conducting affairs has had the beneficial side effect that I appear to have inadvertently immortalised us both with the line "Dr. Livingstone, I presume?"
     I do hope that my delivery of letters from your children has brought you happiness, and I was very

continued overleaf

continued from previous page

pleased to be the first to bring news of the opening of the Suez Canal.

I was particularly impressed to notice that the grey tweed trousers in which you met me had obviously stood up remarkably well to the rigours of the African climate, so could I perhaps ask for details of the cloth and the name of your tailor, as I believe he could make a fortune kitting out expeditions?

While it is unlikely that we will meet again face to face, I do hope that we can continue to correspond through this newfangled email device.

Best wishes,
Henry Morton Stanley

Putting all this into practice might seem a bit daunting and even formulaic, but bear in mind that the four strands we've enumerated above arise out of analysis of good follow-ups. Clearly, if you're in the 'I don't have time for this stuff' camp, then it's going to be difficult to persuade you to take more time and effort to construct personalised follow-ups that require a bit of thought and imagination. But if the alternative is to spend less time doing something that is demonstrably ineffective, then you really have an easy choice to make.

IN A NUTSHELL

A good follow-up can turn a one-off meeting into a more productive relationship.

Having dealt with the content of the follow-up, it's worth thinking about delivery. There was a time when we would have said that the conventional letter was pretty much dead. But, since then, our email boxes have filled with spam and it's increasingly likely that your email will be blocked or deleted without being read. So occasionally, if you really want to make a strong impression, consider writing and posting a real letter.

Sending a follow-up is the visible and public face of the post-meeting work for the committed networker, but there's a lot more that has to go on behind the scenes in terms of recording, organising and storing the information about people you've met.

But what makes up that key information? When we ask that question at workshops, answers fired back at us tend to be the usual suspects: contact details, place of work, job title... Then it all goes quiet, which confirms to us that many people don't think anything like broadly enough about the sort of information that is worth collecting.

CASE STUDY

Tony's Night Out

I was having dinner with a business contact a while back. I'd met him only once before in the office environment, and we agreed to meet for lunch when he was in London. By the time we'd finished the meal, I knew:

■ He liked red wine and didn't drink white

■ He enjoyed badminton

■ He'd damaged his lower back years ago playing squash

■ He'd just got his private pilot's licence

■ He was married

■ He enjoyed wood carving

■ He was 49 and it happened to be his birthday on the day that we had lunch

■ His company's turnover, number of staff and overall plans.

That's the sort of information that none of us can hold in our memories for more than a day or two, at most. If it's not written down somewhere, it's lost.

Now you might think information like that is completely unimportant and the stuff of idle conversation rather than grown-up business. But as we've already said, making people feel good about themselves is an excellent way of getting them on your side... and what better way to make them feel good than to demonstrate that you can remember what they said to you last time you met? Besides, on a very basic level, people like talking about themselves, so its also a great way of staying in touch, striking up a conversation or keeping it going next time you meet in person.

Changing the scenery a bit, you might want to be able to demonstrate recall of who was around the table for a particular dinner, or who was present at a drinks party. You might remember for a day or two the names of the couple you met at Mr X's dinner party, but we absolutely guarantee you won't remember that information longer term unless there was something particularly memorable about either the people or the event.

What happens, then, when you know you're going to bump into the same people again, but you can't for the life of you remember their names? They're probably in the same boat, but if you can walk up to them confidently and address them by name and remember something about them from your last meeting, it makes you look very impressive. It's often said that 'Information is Power', and unless you're lucky enough to have one of those amazing memories that newspaper ads offer you, a first-class database is a good second-best.

IN A NUTSHELL

Your contacts database should be more than just an address book.

It's said that Bill Clinton – who would not have achieved what he has without being an ace networker – got into the habit at the end of each day of filling out an index card for each new person he had met that day, saving personal information about where he had met them, what they did and what they talked about. The story goes that, when he was first running for office, someone at the planning meeting asked where they should start looking for campaign funds. Clinton apparently said "Come with me", and took the questioner to a room stacked to the ceiling with card index boxes. "These are all the people I've ever met since I entered politics," said Clinton. "Why don't we start with them?" The rest, as they say, is history... and if it's good enough for people like Bill Clinton, it's probably a good thing for the rest of us.

DO TRY THIS

Loves Opera, Hates Golf

Think about someone you met for the first time in the last couple of days and quickly jot down a few bullet points about what you can remember of your conversation – however apparently trivial.

Now think back to a similar meeting that took place a couple of months ago and try the same thing.

Which of the two resulted in quicker recall and more bullet points? Almost certainly the first, which shows that we really don't retain 'peripheral' information for very long in our short-term memory.

It really doesn't matter whether you jot that information down on the back of a business card or bus ticket on the way home as long as (a) you do it, and (b) you later put that information into some sort of retrieval system where you can find it quickly and easily. So let's talk a little bit about retrieval systems.

One of the most common excuses we come across is the heartfelt moan "I'm too busy to network." Our answer is that networking is not an optional extra, so you've got to make time for it. On the other hand, though, anything you can do to make your networking quicker and easier must be a good thing. And that's where a digital database comes in.

What you need, put simply, is a retrieval system that enables you to find information quickly and easily. The problem with paper-based systems is they're not hugely portable. They're also not easily searchable. And they're difficult (if not impossible) to back up. Here are a couple of real life examples.

Tony Dons Boater And Blazer

I was entertaining some friends at Henley. It was going to be a nice mix of business and pleasure but, as I drove there, it suddenly dawned on me that I was going to have to make introductions, and that

I simply couldn't remember the names of a couple who were friends of friends and who had been there the previous year and were due to be there again. To be seen not to remember their names would have been unforgivable, so out came the trusty PDA that goes everywhere with me, in went the key word 'Henley' and out came the required names.

What would have happened had Tony not been able to do a digital keyword search? What would have happened if he had not had the discipline or forethought to have entered the couple's names in his database with the note "Met at Henley 2002 – friends of Juliet and Mike" or similar?

Judith Tracks Down Her Man

I was commissioned to create a controlled circulation magazine, and wanted to contact a designer with whom I'd worked on another project several years earlier. I realised that I had completely forgotten his name, and all I could remember about him was that he lived in Cambridge.

I typed Cambridge as a keyword into my contacts database, and up came a short list from which it was easy to see at a glance which was the correct one – instantly refreshing my memory and making me wonder how I could possibly have forgotten his name.

I called the number, found that Mike had moved, but tracked him down with one more call and updated my database accordingly.

Technology has a huge amount to offer networkers, but whatever whizzy device or applications you're using, the old rule 'garbage in, garbage out' most definitely applies, so ask yourself two questions. What information is important to me? And how do I want it to look?

First, we need to make sure we are capturing the right information about our contacts from the outset. If we capture only partial information, that ultimately costs us time and hassle because, at the very point when we want to contact someone, we find that we're missing their mobile number or their postal address.

Second, think about the device you're using and the software. Rather than just accepting the default field names and sizes offered by your software and then realising after you've entered 100 names that you should have set it up differently, it's worth spending a little while thinking about the set up. If that means buying additional or replacement software that offers greater functionality than the original, the result will more than compensate. The whole point of getting your contact management system set up correctly is just that... management: the ability not only to conjure up any contact's details and history at the tap of a few keys but also to do something useful with that information.

There are clearly an enormous number of ever-changing permutations for hardware and software, so, rather than make recommendations about the technology, we'll give you some pointers of the features to look out for, based on our experience over the years with a large number of PIMs (personal information managers), CRMs (customer relationship managers) and devices.

1. The ability to view, wherever possible, all data from one record on the same screen

2. The ability to add extra, non-standard fields (for example, you could add a field for the secretary's name – that way you're less likely to forget to ask)

3. Configurable, free form notes field(s) capable of accepting everything you might want to jot down about that person

4. Comprehensive search facility for a whole word or part of a word in any field

5. Filters that allow you to select a subset of your contact data (for example, only those for whom you have an email address)

6. Multiple category management that allows you to group people by defined criteria (for example, people you went to business school with, or members of your choir)

7. Connectivity to other computers

8. Upgradeability, backward compatibility... staying power!

9. Easy and complete backup.

Our suggestion is that you keep your primary contact database on your laptop or desktop, which is likely to offer powerful, fully featured programs, and synchronise this regularly with a handheld device that can travel with you and act both as an extension of your own memory and as a handy post-meeting jotter for key information.

It's also worth spending a few moments looking at the ownership and stewardship of data. Every so often, we come across someone who declaims (sometimes almost proudly) that they don't have to worry about managing contact data because their boss actually deals with all the client contacts, or because their PA inputs it all on the company system when handed a bunch of business cards after a meeting.

But what happens if the well-networked boss gets run over by a bus or you arrive one morning to find your desk has been cleared? How can you expect to develop your own network if you constantly rely on someone else's?

With or without administrative help inputting basic data, you are the only person who can really manage your contact data and ensure that the sort of information that you personally will find useful is included. But there are two potential 'gotchas'.

The first relates to ownership of data. If you were to arrive at work tomorrow morning to find a burly security guard barring your way, and the contents of your desk in a box by the reception desk, would you still have access to the contact data that you have faithfully entered on the firm's central CRM system? Almost certainly not, and it is a moot point as to whether that contact data is owned by the company (on whose time you presumably made those contacts) or by you, who actually made the connection.

Either way, if the only place that data is stored is on the company system, then it would be lost to you, with perhaps several years of contact data suddenly inaccessible. We're not advocating taking an 'off-site backup' of the firm's data, but you should perhaps consider whether you store information about contacts you have made personally somewhere that is guaranteed to be available whatever happens in the future.

The second data protection issue relates to the sort of information you store. Paradoxically, the most useful personal data can often be exactly that which you probably wouldn't want your subject to see if they demanded and got access to their record on your company's CRM system. So if you're going to store personal information about people (and especially if you're going to include debatable or controversial value judgements about them as well as facts), then you should consider using your own contact management system in parallel.

If you wouldn't want your contacts to see that data, what about other prying eyes? Laptops and handhelds routinely get stolen and office based machines are an easy target for walk-in thieves. Having your sensitive contact data in their grubby hands is probably not a good idea, so it's well worth password protecting your contact management program as well as your computer logon.

Let's close this chapter – for a reason you'll see in a moment – with a question whose answer never ceases to amaze us. Is all your contact data backed up?

The fact is that every single reader of this book has a contact network that is unique to them and that has been built up over the years. It's a valuable, unique and very personal resource. If that information was to vanish, it would be impossible to reinstate it in its original form: any attempt to do so would, in most cases, be incredibly time consuming and a pale imitation of the richness of the original data.

CASE STUDY

You Won't Miss It 'Til It's Gone!

As we got a workshop under way, we were aware that one of the booked participants hadn't arrived. Half way through the morning, the missing delegate turned up looking tired and fraught, made his apologies and took his seat.

Later in the day, we came on to the subject of contact and data management, and asked if everybody had their data backed up. There was a groan from the front row as our late arrival volunteered that "The reason I was late was because my hard disk crashed yesterday evening. I was up until three in the morning trying to rescue stuff, but I've lost it all and it wasn't backed up. I just wish your workshop had been a day earlier!"

Don't assume that your data is safe just because the company routinely runs a system backup: many such routines will back up data on the central server but will not back up data held on local machines. Nor should you be sitting there smugly just because you've eschewed the newfangled computer idea and keep all your data in business card books and Rolodexes that patently don't need backing up. Rubbish... never heard of fire or flood? It's the easiest thing in the world to photocopy a business card book and keep the copies off site, and only marginally more fiddly to do the same thing with a Rolodex.

IN A NUTSHELL

Back up your contact data completely and frequently.

Well, that's the reason we left data backup until last: no excuse not to go and back up your data right now and not go on to the next chapter until you've done so.

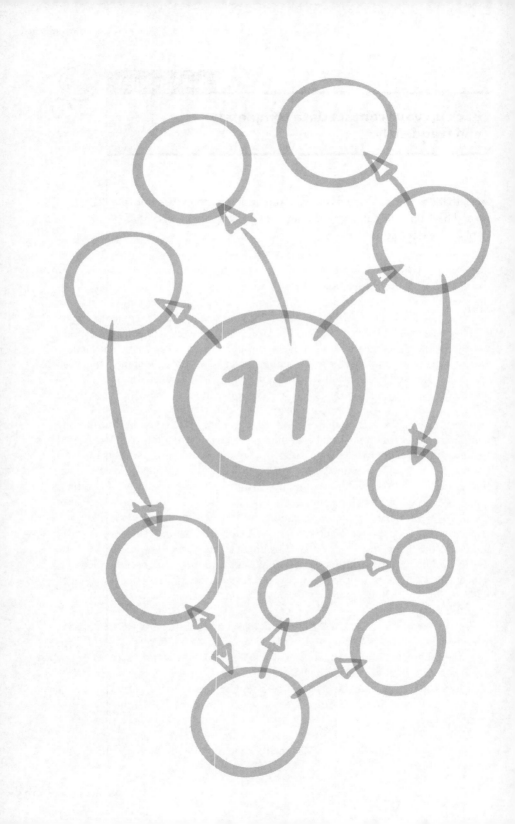

CHAPTER ELEVEN

I Saw This and Thought of You

"Now, here, you see, it takes all the running
you can do to stay in the same place. If you
want to get somewhere else, you must run
twice as fast as that."

LEWIS CARROLL *Through The Looking Glass*

How many names do you have in your database, business card book or Rolodex? If you've never counted, now might be a good time to do so, as a reminder of just how well connected you could be if you took the trouble. The chances are that you'll have hundreds of names in there – some of which you'll frown at and wonder who they are; others you might remember fondly but haven't thought about in years. And the question in your mind, no doubt, is "How on earth do I stay in touch with all these people?"

Before we begin to answer that question, however, let's step back and consider an even more fundamental question: "Why bother to stay in touch?" The following two case studies may help provide an answer.

CASE STUDY

It's A Marathon, Not A Sprint

Some time ago, we ran a workshop for a top law firm. One of the senior partners was himself an ace networker but thankfully still seemed to be getting something useful out of what we were teaching! (As an aside, we sometimes get better feedback on our workshops from the more senior and more mature participants than we do from younger or more junior people. Our reading of this phenomenon is that those who have been around a bit know that, however good they are, they can always pick up a useful tip or strengthen an area of weakness. Only those who don't know what they don't know really think they know it all.)

But back to the story. Our senior partner related his own experience of having started out as an articled clerk. Doing a lot of conveyancing work for corporate clients, he found himself working quite frequently with a trainee surveyor in a well-known commercial estate agency, and the two men became friends as well as colleagues.

Our articled clerk rose through the ranks, staying put in one firm. His surveyor friend, on the other hand, moved companies from time to time, achieving advancement with each move and, crucially, staying in touch. Not only did the two men continue to work together but, in each new position, the surveyor introduced our solicitor to new work colleagues who were themselves potential new clients for legal services.

Both men are now in senior positions in their respective professions. They have been friends and colleagues for over 20 years and still work together. That's great, but it's only part of the picture: more interestingly, our solicitor has not just continued to work with this one surveyor but has been introduced to, and cultivated, new business contacts in every one of the half dozen companies through which his friend has passed.

CASE STUDY

A Stitch In Time (Saves Nine)

Kathryn is an accountant by profession. She qualified in 1979 and, after a year or two with a large firm, she moved to a smaller company based in Surrey in order to broaden her experience:

"I've always known that raising my profile and visibility was going to be important to my career. So when I moved to Surrey, I made a point of joining the local Chartered Accountants' Group. Through the Group, of which I later became Chair, I was able to establish a wide network of other accountants – self-employed, working for other accountancy firms, and people working in industry.

"I got married in 1982 and knew that I wanted to start a family

continued overleaf

continued from previous page

and keep my hand in professionally. So I looked around for interests that might enable me to work from home. I started writing and marking exams for the Institute of Chartered Accountants, and gradually got involved in the Institute's scheme for accrediting firms to train student accountants. As well as forcing me to keep up to date with developments in my profession, it also meant that I had to attend occasional training courses, editorial meetings and so forth. So I got out and about a little which made a welcome change from childcare and marking exam papers.

"I also joined the Women in Accountancy Group, which helped me build my network among women accountants, work for a cause I believed in – and have a lot of fun, as well!

"As a result of all this, I maintained and even extended my network and kept up to date. Over the years, I also made a point of keeping in touch with people whom I trained and worked with in my first job, all those years ago. Many of them have become good friends, as well as sources of work.

"When I was ready to go back to full-time employment, I didn't suffer from a lack of confidence after six years at home. And, funnily enough, it was through my examinations work that I was invited to join one of the major firms of chartered accountants and eventually became the head of a large national team of forensic accountants."

These case studies illustrate key networking principles that we'll look at in this chapter: the importance of staying in touch, and the critical role played by the referral process in expanding your network.

It might sound like a contradiction in terms, but it's never too late to start staying in touch and everything we say here applies not just to maintaining existing contacts but also to the process of actively looking for ways to re-establish links with old acquaintances and lapsed friends. One habit we particularly want to break at the outset is the frame of mind that says "I can't possibly phone so-and-so because I haven't spoken to them for years." We realise that we're not going to change the mindset of a lifetime without some strong evidence, so how about this for starters.

CASE STUDY

Just Do It!

Helen tells us that, before our networking workshop, she wouldn't have dared pick up the phone to someone she hadn't seen or spoken to for five years. After the workshop, her thinking had changed to the point where she asked herself "What's the worst thing that could happen?"

She told herself to have courage and picked up the phone to an old friend. "She was really pleased to hear from me and had also been wondering what had happened to me," reports Helen. "It seemed as though the years had vanished, we agreed to meet up and talked for hours just catching up on our lives. While we don't see each other that often we have stayed in touch since then and when we do get together it always feels like we last saw each other only a week ago.

"The workshop gave me the confidence to make that original call and that has led to greater confidence to 'make the call' more generally. I have expanded my network as a result and made and kept in contact with people who have helped me in both a personal and professional capacity."

It's also worth remembering that 'it takes two to tango' – that is, losing touch requires inaction on the part of both parties, so unless the person that you're attempting to reconnect with has persistently failed to respond to emails, texts and phone calls, it's reasonable to assume that the blame is evenly spread, and the chances are that they will be as happy to hear from you as you are to connect with them.

If you're still not convinced, just think for a moment about how quickly life happens and how key life events (good and bad) occupy your time and attention. So, although you haven't been in touch with someone for 5, 10 or even 30 years (see the next case study), the reality is that you've both been occupied elsewhere and the time has probably flown by.

Of course, it's easy to trot out the slogan "Just Do It", but that's actually very misleading – nobody 'just' learns to ride a unicyle or to juggle chainsaws, and we're the first to admit that 'just' getting back into contact with someone takes nerve and determination. But once you've taken the plunge and discovered that not only have you not died of embarrassment but that you've also made a successful and interesting reconnection, you'll find yourself much more prepared to give it a go in future. If you're still in doubt, ask yourself "What's the worst thing that can happen?" The answer: silence.

IN A NUTSHELL

Don't discard people you haven't been in touch with recently. Instead, actively seek out and reconnect with lapsed contacts.

What we've said previously about the importance of chance encounters in taking you in new directions or bringing you new information has an interesting echo here too. Most of us will have had the experience of passing someone in the street whom we recognise from our past. Sometimes we smile wanly, other times we are careful not to make eye contact in order to avoid a potential encounter, and sometimes we're 100 yards down the road before we actually register who they are and where we know them from.

But next time it happens to you, see it not as an opportunity for embarrassment or a potential delay in your already busy day but as a chance to reconnect with a 'weak tie' acquaintance. You never know, they might even turn into a friend, and it's quite amazing how some people you had absolutely no time for at school (or vice versa) can mature into decent human beings.

CASE STUDY

Tony Finds That Phil Hasn't Changed A Bit

My wife's train from London was severely delayed from its usual arrival time of 9 pm, and I found myself still hanging around at Newcastle station at 10.30 pm. Sitting in the car, I listened to the radio and 'people watched' as the clock moved slowly towards the new arrival time.

Suddenly, in the half light of the station car park, I spotted a profile that I recognised, helping a young woman with her baggage. It looked like Phil, a very good school friend whom I hadn't seen since we were 17 years old. "Can't be," was my first thought, as the Phil I knew was based in West London.

But Phil would be the first to agree that he has quite memorable features, and I was sure it was him, even after a gap of thirty years; however, if it wasn't, it would be embarrassing all round. So what to do? I could simply watch this person drive away, and that would be that. Or I could find some way of approaching someone who could turn out to be a complete stranger.

In a flash of inspiration, it occurred to me that I could just call out his name – if it was him, he'd turn round. If it wasn't, he wouldn't (unless I was very unlucky and the stranger also happened to be called Phil...).

So I called out "Phil!" and he looked round. It was indeed him, and he was at Newcastle station to collect his daughter. It turned out that he had lived in the area for many years, half an hour's drive from us, and we're now firmly back in contact.

Here again we have networking operating on both a 'targeted' and 'diffuse' level: 'targeted' when we want to reconnect with someone from our past because we have something to offer them or something we want from them; and 'diffuse' when reconnecting with someone just because we have the opportunity to do so, with no preconception as to where that might take us. Either way, what we're doing is re-establishing some 'weak ties' that can extend the reach and diversity of our network.

But what can we do to avoid losing touch in the first place with the hundreds or even thousands of people we have in our address books?

The first hurdle to navigate is the common complaint that "I don't have time to stay in touch with all these people." So, before looking at specifics, let's revisit the issue of how we store our contact information. We talked in the previous chapter about the importance of a good contact management system, and it's in staying in touch over the longer term that a well-designed system really comes into its own. If you didn't get the point when we made it earlier, your contact management system can be so much more than a passive address book or phone list, but only if you enter the right information, store it in an accessible format, and know how to make use of it.

If you've set up your contact management system to have an internal logic that's right for your network, then it's possible with just a few mouse clicks to send the same (or a personalised) email to everyone in your database or to any given subset, to create reminders of people's birthdays or anniversaries, and to keep the right people posted about key events in your personal or professional life.

IN A NUTSHELL

If you think you don't have time to stay in touch, get organised and *make* time!

From a networking standpoint, there's a real skill in finding reasons and opportunities to stay in touch with people. Let's be clear, we're not talking about 'spamming' them, but about sending them something they might actually want to receive.

OK, they might or might not be interested in that 'round robin' you send out at Christmas to let them know just how well your kids are doing at school and that the new dog is almost housetrained, but you can be much more creative and selective in what you send people.

DO TRY THIS

Any Excuse?

Think about some of the people you wish you had stayed in touch with. Pick a couple of names, and make a list of the possible reasons you could use to send them an email, write a note, or pick up the phone.

Now compare your list with our own starter list of ten excuses for making contact. And then, of course, get out your pen and paper, or put your finger on your mouse, and start getting in touch!

1. The appointments column. Every industry and profession has at least one magazine carrying news of appointments and promotions. If you see someone you know mentioned, what a great opportunity to drop them a line and congratulate them (or commiserate!).

2. The quoted expert. If you see someone you know quoted in print or making a media appearance, use the opportunity to congratulate them on their profile and visibility.

3. The festive card. Tried and tested, Christmas, Eid, Diwali, and Hanukah cards are a classic way of staying in touch, and a good database makes the whole process a piece of cake. But do make sure that your signature is legible. And if your name is David, or Mary, or any other relatively everyday name, do make sure that your surname appears somewhere, so the recipient can identify you.

4. The 'this reminded me of you' note. Whether it's a place you visited together, a conference you both attended or something to do with that person's hobbies and interests, anything that makes you think of that other person is a perfect (and flattering) excuse to get in touch.

continued overleaf

continued from previous page

5. The interesting snippet. You read something that could provide useful intelligence or just interesting reading for someone you know. Why not scan it and email it across to them with a 'thought this might interest you' note? And if you found the article on the internet, then use that wonderful 'send this to a friend' button.

6. The introduction. We talked in Chapter 2 about the invaluable role that connectors play in networking. So even if you're not naturally one of life's connectors, that's no excuse for not making an effort to put people in touch with each other – perhaps because they work in the same industry, or have similar interests.

7. The request for help. We've said it before, and we'll say it again: asking for help is a sign of strength, not weakness. After all, in this age of information overload, nobody can know everything they need to do their job – and few of us will do the same job for our entire careers. So when faced with an issue or a dilemma, turn to your most valuable and personal resource: your network.

8. The invitation. If you're organising, or just attending, a conference, why not get in touch with a few colleagues and see if they're also planning to go. Often, the most valuable part of a conference or exhibition isn't the formal proceedings but the informal chats in coffee breaks or in the aisles.

9. The update. If done badly, repeated self-congratulatory emails from people boasting about their achievements can irritate. But if done well, a succinct note telling people about a change in circumstances (new job, promotion, start or completion of studies, the arrival of a child, etc., etc.) helps to keep your contacts up to date with what you're up to.

10. The joke. A word of caution here: don't use too freely, or you'll find your emails reclassified as spam. But the occasional well-chosen joke can enliven a colleague's day.

With just a little effort and creativity on your part, you should be able to double or treble this list with ideas that are applicable and appropriate to your own personality and your own network. In fact, if challenged about ways to stay in touch, we'd say "Any excuse". But remember, the whole point of the exercise is to remind people of your existence, and to ensure that they regard your communication in a positive light, one that enhances rather than detracts from your reputation. Here's a good example.

CASE STUDY

Judith Receives A Blast From The Past

Here's an email I received a while back from Shivani, a designer I had worked with back in my publishing days:

Hi Judith!
How are you? Remember me from our days at XYZ Publishing?!

I was just going through some old paperwork getting organised and found your contact details, just had to say hello.

Hope you are well... what are you doing these days? I'm trying to survive in the world of freelance design – juggling a million and one things. We never did have that coffee get together...

Get in touch, would be great to catch up.

Best wishes
Shivani

I was delighted to hear from her – we had always got on extremely well, and I just happened to have a project that was right up Shivani's street.

In convincing yourself to find the time to do some of this stuff, you need to make sure you're looking down the right end of the telescope: it doesn't matter whether the recipient of that 'saw this and thought of you' email has already seen that interesting snippet. The point is that, by sending it, you have reminded them of your existence and have shown yourself to have been thinking of them – the reinforcement of a weak tie and a psychological compliment in one go.

Shivani had the nerve to get in touch after a gap of several years knowing that the very worst that could happen was a complete lack of response. And she didn't feel the need to manufacture an excuse for getting in touch but was able to subtly say that she was looking for work (by mentioning her new freelance status). The result was another client for her freelance portfolio.

A quick word here about the all-pervasiveness of email and the way that most people these days default to email or text message. If you stop to consider the vast quantity of email that most of us have to deal with, you may start to question whether it's always the best form of communication. Sometimes, picking up the phone or sending something in the post might be more effective.

But it's very much 'horses for courses' and we encourage you to think actively about what, how and why you're communicating. For example, sending someone 'hard copy' of an interesting article by post will probably grab their attention more quickly and certainly than sending it by email, which then requires it to be read on screen or printed out.

Then think of the Christmas card, which some corporates, charities and individuals send out by the thousand. Apart from the fact that the signature on some of those cards is illegible (and what on earth is the point of sending someone a card if the recipient can't work out who it's from?), those cards arrive in a deluge at a time of year when the recipient is least likely to really appreciate the contact.

Why not think laterally and do something different to make yourself stand out from the crowd?

CASE STUDY

Proverbial Postcards

Every year we choose a relevant (and, we hope, fun) aphorism that we've come across in our travels, and print a postcard bearing the words of wisdom.

We've found that sending out these postcards elicits a really positive response. We often see them pinned to people's notice boards, stuck to the filing cabinet or propped up on their desk. And, invariably, our card prompts one or more people to get in touch again.

If you want to be prosperous for a year, grow grain.

If you want to be prosperous for ten years, grow trees.

If you want to be prosperous for a lifetime, grow people.

Chinese proverb

—*Management Advantage* —

www.manadvan.com

I find that the harder I work, the more luck I seem to have.

Thomas Jefferson (1743-1826)

www.manadvan.com

—*Management Advantage* —

A desk is a dangerous place from which to watch the world.

John Le Carré, 'The Honourable Schoolboy'

www.manadvan.com

—*Management Advantage* —

If you do what you've always done,

you'll get what you always got...

—*Management Advantage* —

www.manadvan.com

IN A NUTSHELL

Think laterally and creatively about ways of staying in touch with your contacts.

Not only are we more geographically mobile than ever before, it's also easier than ever to discard one phone number or email address for another when a better deal comes along or a contract ends. You might think you'd never let that happen, but we know from the experience of working with many alumni groups that the 'bounce' rate for emails is enormous.

All too often that means missed opportunities. Throughout this book we've touched on the importance of referrals in the networking process – we see them as the 'engine' or powerhouse of networking. If you've ever had to make cold calls (and who hasn't?), then you'll be fully aware of what a soul-destroying activity it can be. If, instead, you can 'warm up' a cold call by telling the person that "Alexander gave me your name" or "Joanne thought it might be worth speaking to you", not only is the call much easier to make but it's also much more likely to be successful.

Why? Because of what we call the 'obligation phenomenon'. Imagine yourself on the receiving end of such a phone call. What do you do? If you effectively tell the caller to get lost, how will you explain this to the friend/acquaintance/colleague who gave them your name? "Sorry mate, I just couldn't be bothered?" Uncomfortable, at best; downright embarrassing at worst.

Alternatively, you could take the call, listen to what they have to say, and then decide whether or not you're able (or willing) to help. Whatever you decide, you can honestly tell the referrer that you were delighted to help or that you gave them a hearing but weren't able to come up with what they wanted.

In other words, a referral more or less obliges the recipient of the call to at least give you a hearing. And you can't ask for more than that from your networking activity.

Here's an example of somebody who leaned this lesson the hard way.

Hunting Heads

Christian was job-hunting. He collected the names of 150 head-hunters and started cold calling. Although he spoke to 20 almost immediately, he was discouraged because he couldn't get through to the vast majority. Most didn't answer their own phones, didn't respond to voicemail messages, didn't return calls, or relied on an obstructive secretary to effectively block access.

Nevertheless, he persevered, spending an astonishing six to eight hours a day, over two months, on the phone. In the end, he managed to speak to all but seven of them, and got meetings with about ten (less than 8%).

Then he had a brainwave. As an alumnus of London Business School, he had access to the School alumni directory, and managed to find 47 people working in HR and recruitment. He called them all and, if he didn't get through first time, he left a very straightforward message: "I'm a fellow LBS alum – I'd like some career advice."

The difference was miraculous. He managed to speak to all of them (except two) within a few days and had exploratory interviews with ten (over 20%). All were friendly and helpful. One sent a list of personal contacts in the industry and Christian used his name as a door opener. Another spent two hours with him on a visit to London from Newcastle, going through his CV and coming up with ideas for approaching companies.

Christian's verdict: "Amazing!"

The fact that a warm call is almost invariably more productive than a cold call isn't rocket science. Yet it took Christian two months to realise that there was a way round the brick wall. So instead of giving yourself a headache, try to find a smart way round the obstacle rather than continuing to bang your head against it.

However, do beware of the contact who says "You ought to speak to so-and-so. I'll give them a call for you." Sometimes, they may do just that. But what if they fail to deliver? If you can get the contact details and make the call yourself, you stay in control of the transaction. You know the call will be made because you'll be making it, and you know what will be said because you'll be saying it.

And always get permission from the 'referrer' to mention their name, as the following case illustrates.

CASE STUDY

Fools Rush In

Gemma, a young lawyer interested in environmental law, asked for advice from her mentor, Derek.

"He told me to speak to John, James, Sarah and Margaret, and generously gave me their contact details. They were all specialists and extremely knowledgeable and, he was sure, would be willing to help out with some advice and information.

"I was keen to rush off to make my phone calls, assuming naively that they would fall over themselves to talk to me once they heard that Derek had put me in touch. But Derek said 'Hang on a moment. By all means use my name when making contact – except, that is, when you get in touch with Margaret. She and I had a pretty serious falling out last year, and I doubt if mentioning my name will do you any favours.'

"Thank goodness Derek was my mentor, and thoughtful enough to warn me. A less kind person could have just left me to learn the hard way."

IN A NUTSHELL

Giving and receiving referrals is a cornerstone of the networking process. Staying in touch keeps your address book up to date, and makes sure that people know how to find you.

To sum up, remember that staying in touch with people over the long term involves 'playing a long game' and realising that you never know exactly where life will take you, and when you might need a helping hand from your friends (and acquaintances).

Effective networking is a career-long, not to say life-long, set of behaviours and you have to be honest enough to recognise that, however special you think you are, you are probably not going to be 'front of mind' very often, or for very long, with 'weak tie' acquaintances who have their own busy lives to lead.

So making it easy for other people to find you is half the battle. The other half involves actively reminding them who you are and where you are. Do it little and often rather than overwhelming them with stuff, and do vary your methods.

Finally, reminding people about your existence (and indeed, what you're doing and where you are at this very minute) is something that has been transformed by the 'social networking' phenomenon. So much so that your reputation can stand or fall on what you say about yourself, and what gets said about you online, and that's what we'll deal with in the final chapter.

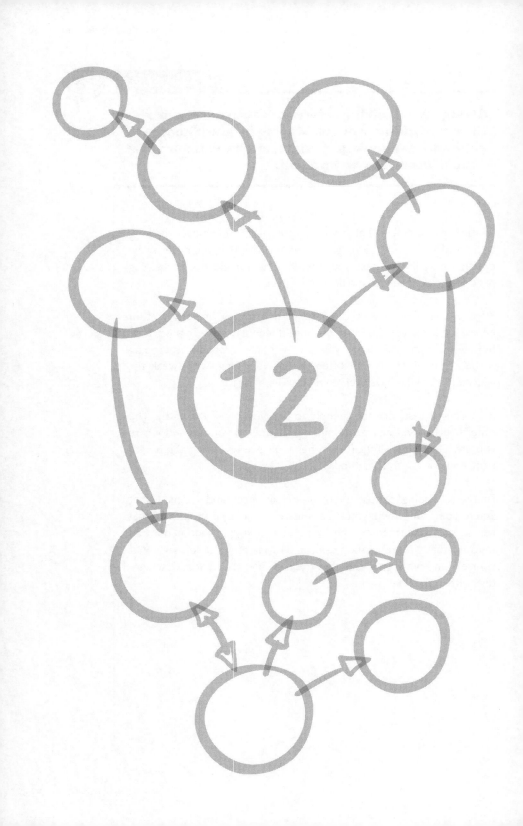

CHAPTER TWELVE

Social Networking, Your Network and Your Reputation

It is not good enough to have a good aim in life – you've got to pull the trigger!

ANON

The reason that we've left discussion of reputation until the very end is that your reputation is actually the synthesis of everything else we've put into this book: it's what the people around you really think of you, and what they'll tell others in the network about you that they perhaps might not say to your face. A truly effective network, then, is perhaps one in which your (positive) reputation goes before you.

So, just as there are things you can do to enhance your networking effectiveness, there are things you can do to maintain and enhance your reputation. Oscar Wilde may have said "There's only one thing worse than being talked about, and that's not being talked about" but, as the following case study shows, a reputation can easily be trashed and you may be the last person to know it's happened.

CASE STUDY

Her Reputation Arrived Before She Did

A participant at an 'in house' corporate workshop told us about Amanda (not her real name), who had managed to pull off the difficult trick of being both a lazy and inefficient manager and an argumentative and difficult subordinate.

As was pointed out by one participant (with nods of agreement from others), such people have a knack of 'knowing their rights' without addressing the other side of the deal and delivering on their responsibilities. They're also notorious for being difficult to dislodge from the management hierarchy... so one answer is to shift them sideways to make them someone else's problem.

And that's what happened here, but the 'grapevine' being what it is, everyone in Amanda's new section knew exactly what she was like before she even walked through the door. Even if she'd recognised her faults (or had them pointed out by her boss) and wanted to start afresh and mend her ways, she was faced with an uphill struggle because her new staff were already fatally prejudiced against her.

That story had been told, repeated and embellished at water coolers and coffee machines right across the company. Now, in a workshop setting, the laughter and knowing nods around the table that accompanied its telling demonstrated that Amanda's reputation was trashed beyond salvation.

What's more, given the degree of mobility of staff within and between companies, it's quite likely that Amanda's reputation will precede her wherever she goes next.

Here's a nice counter to that, which may be apocryphal (we can't trace it back to its original source) but the sentiment of active reputation management certainly provides food for thought.

CASE STUDY

When I Was A Lad, I Served A Term...

Two naval cadets met on their first day at Dartmouth Naval College, and became firm friends as they worked their way through the gruelling course. On graduation day, before going to their new postings, John and Ian made a pact that they would each do whatever they could to enhance the other's reputation.

Over the years, the pact did its work. If John was at a meeting or in a wardroom or bar where Ian's name was mentioned, John would make a point of letting people know that Ian was a good person to know, and good at his job. And Ian did the same for John, such that the other's reputation would get a bit of a burnish at every available (and appropriate) opportunity.

By the time they retired, both men had attained senior 'flag' rank in their Service.

Did their active 'reputation management' pact play a part in that success, or would they have attained that rank anyway? Perhaps the very fact that they dreamed up the pact in the first place indicates that, right from the outset, they both had what it took to get a seat at the highest table.

The territory we're into here is that of personal brand management and the value that comes from others in your network providing what in PR terms is known as 'third party credibility'. What you say about yourself is easily and obviously discounted, but what others say about you has real weight.

And this is where 'social networking' sites come into the equation, because never before have we laid our lives so bare for others to see. In many ways, that's a good thing, because we know that recruiters successfully use sites such as LinkedIn to find suitable candidates. On the flip side, it also allows those candidates easy access to much better and more complete information than ever before about possible suitor companies. Online networking gives them a direct line with current and ex-employees, to ask "What's company X *really* like to work for?"

But we also know that recruiters, HR departments and others increasingly screen social networking sites to find out if the CV and the formal interview really match the person they're thinking of hiring. The internet abounds with examples (many astoundingly stupid) of people who have come unstuck because of something they've posted on Facebook or similar; but we use the one below because it is well documented and was widely reported, and because it blighted someone's career.

CASE STUDY

Facebook Lost Policeman Top Job

The following story, taken from the BBC news website, shows how a senior police officer lost out on the chance to become a Chief Inspector after he was found to have posted very personal information on the internet.

"Insp D., British Transport Police's head of royalty and government protection, was offered the job with Bedfordshire Police.

"But when his prospective employer ran background checks it found he had been given a warning over his Facebook page.

"Bedfordshire Police then withdrew the offer to Insp D.

"In a statement Bedfordshire Police told the BBC: 'After the interview (on 13 February) we ran routine background checks and we were told he had a live sanction against him.

"'Therefore we felt unable to proceed with the job offer.'

"The warning had been given to Insp D. by his employers after it was discovered that his page on the social networking website Facebook included graphic details about his gay lifestyle and photographs showing him posing in his uniform at a London tube station."

The central issue here is not the lifestyle but the judgement shown by the officer in making "graphic details" available online and "posing in his uniform". We've heard of another case in which a job offer was withdrawn because the recruiter decided, after looking at the potential employee's Facebook page, that the candidate had a recreational drug habit, and so was unsuitable for the post.

Our online presence and reputation is so important these days that it even has a name – our 'NetRep' – and a new wave of entrepreneurs offering to clean it up for us, because even if we remove that embarrassing photo or unguarded comment from our own or a social networking website, it's likely that the offending item will remain 'cached' and available for retrieval.

IN A NUTSHELL

If you wouldn't want it made public, don't put it in a public place.

Having dealt with the downsides, let's see what can we do about enhancing our reputation online. Limiting this to a purely networking perspective, there is a great opportunity to use the web to garner testimonials and recommendations from others about your past work.

The trouble is that even those of us who should know better find it difficult to ask.

Tony Learns That 'If You Ask, You Get'

I was doing some 'housekeeping' on LinkedIn, where Management Advantage operates a group open primarily to those who have attended our workshops, and suddenly realised that, although many people have emailed us over the years to say how useful and/or enjoyable they'd found our workshop, that information wasn't visible to others.

We were clearly missing an opportunity to manage our reputations online, especially as LinkedIn makes it so easy to "Request a Recommendation" from anyone you're directly connected to.

But somehow the idea of actually asking for a recommendation seemed distasteful, and I spent some time pondering just what it was that made me so reluctant to ask. After all, if we were good, people would say so of their own accord... wouldn't they? And there was the answer. I'd been looking at things through the wrong end of the telescope. If people didn't know that a LinkedIn recommendation would be useful and valuable to us, how would they know to provide one unless asked?

Still feeling slightly uncomfortable, I selected all my LinkedIn contacts as recipients of the request, and pressed 'Send'.

Within 24 hours, I had 20 great recommendations back out of the 158 requests I'd sent – a 'hit' rate of 12.5%. Where appropriate, those recommendations provided me with the opportunity and momentum to return the favour, but the really interesting thing is that some of the recommendations received were from people I'd not communicated with recently, offering me a fantastic opportunity to reconnect to some of those 'weak ties' we mention so often.

Those recommendations are now visible to all on LinkedIn. They were all given willingly and, as far as I know, genuinely represent the view of their authors.

So do be prepared to ask. But what of the 'missing' 88.5% non-respondents in this case study? Some won't have felt inclined or informed enough to provide a recommendation, others will have changed their email addresses and never seen the request. Others still (and a straw poll of recipients suggests this was quite common) did something that we've warned against before in these pages when talking about 'following up' and actively responding to requests for help: they read the request and moved on, intending to come back to it later but never actually doing so.

IN A NUTSHELL

Tell people what you want to happen, because they're not mind readers.

As we bring this chapter, and the book, to a close, we'd like to share a case study that shows how the consummate networker manages to make connections, think laterally and expand their network while also both giving and receiving. It's a snapshot of almost everything we've dealt with so far.

CASE STUDY

Jeremy In Action

"I attended an Oxford Business Alumni event at Horseguards Barracks in Hyde Park and met a woman named Rebecca. We chatted and we got on well: I was working on my MBA and she was in the process of applying to MBA programs. She mentioned her strong interest in the Kellogg School of Management. I

continued overleaf

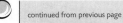

continued from previous page

mentioned that my cousin Mike had gone there and probably wouldn't mind telling her about it.

"Next day, we exchanged 'great to meet you' emails, and a few weeks later she wrote to ask for Mike's details. I sent an email to Mike cc'ing Rebecca. They got in touch and she ended up getting into Kellogg.

"Quite separately, I met Judith at a Management Advantage workshop. She mentioned that she'd worked in branding, which I was planning to get into post MBA, so I followed up with her soon afterwards. She responded by sending me an article with rankings of branding consultancies. The article contained an inset graphic for Workthing.com, with a caption that Workthing had used a branding agency to devise its identity.

"Then the light bulb went on: Rebecca from the Horseguards event was head of Workthing. So I emailed Rebecca saying: 'I saw this article...would you be willing to share your branding consultancy contacts?'

"Rebecca's reply contained four names and email addresses of the people who had pitched for the Workthing business. I wrote to them in turn, working Rebecca's referral into a pretty damn good cover letter and talking about my interest in their branding and requesting a meeting at which I might pick their brains (nothing about how I'm looking for a job, other than something about how 'I'm finishing up my MBA').

"I got 4 replies:

■ Reply #1: 'Don't remember Rebecca, but you sound interesting and funny. Let's meet.' End result was that I found a mentor, and may yet get work at that company.

■ Reply #2: 'Let's meet, sure.' End result was a two-month contract position doing exactly what I want to be doing, and which may lead to further work with the company.

■ **Reply #3:** Her email's no good anymore and phone calls to her company reveal that she's left and no one knows where. End result: about 30 wasted minutes.

■ **Reply #4:** 'Sure I can meet with you. We don't have any work, but I can give you some advice.' End result was a meeting where I got that advice. It didn't go any further, but I saw the inside of one more branding agency.

"Rebecca is now halfway through her first year at Kellogg, and I'm still making use of the contacts she provided. I also remember her mentioning a long time ago that she had a friend in the publishing business. Even back then I had the stirrings of a book inside me, but they weren't far enough along to mention to any publishers. A couple of weeks ago, though, they got to that point. I looked up Rebecca's student email on the Kellogg website and emailed her again with a newsy email in which I said that I was now ready to take her up on her kind offer of an introduction to publisher friend Dan. She replied with a chatty email of her own and said 'I've written to Dan about you just now. If he doesn't contact you, follow up with him by email.'

"I certainly will."

Let's pick apart the mindset and actions exhibited in this case study to reprise the themes of our previous chapters.

1. Jeremy opts to attend a workshop on networking, even though it's obvious to us that he was already pretty well attuned to the benefits of effective networking. All of us can benefit from learning a few new tricks, or honing existing skills. Once you 'switch on' to the way that good things can flow out of a well nurtured and maintained network, you'll grab any opportunity to put your own skills into action.

2. He understands the value of giving (in this case, a contact who might be able to help someone out with an unbiased opinion about a business school), and delivers on that promise.

3. He also knows that putting people in touch with each other (acting as a 'connector') makes everybody richer.

4. He's not afraid to ask for help. He wanted to get into branding, and asked anybody and everybody if they could provide him with information, advice and referrals. But he also recognises that there are limits: he deliberately doesn't ask for a job, knowing that doing so might reduce his chance of getting a meeting. Instead, he asks if he can 'pick their brains', paying them the psychological compliment that they know more than he does. Almost everybody responds positively to being asked to share their wisdom with a lesser being.

5. He intuitively realises that the basis of any good relationship involves being interested and interesting. So he constructs chatty emails that people will be happy to receive and read.

6. He knows that some contacts or meetings may end up being a 'waste of time'. But he doesn't know which ones, so he does them all rather than risk making wrong assumptions at the outset.

7. Even though he'd lost touch with Rebecca when she went to Kellogg, he had the imagination to do a little research, find her email address and get in touch again rather than let the connection wither.

We sincerely hope that, having read this book, you'll put our ideas into practice. Some of the practical suggestions we've made may be difficult at first, but they will get easier, more comfortable and more natural. We know because we've watched it happen, and we've experienced it ourselves. You'll very soon find that you can network anywhere, anytime and with almost anybody.

We'd genuinely love to hear about your networking successes, failures, triumphs and embarrassments: we all have them and they can all teach someone else a useful lesson.

Whether it's something that happened to you (or someone you know) before reading this book, or something you did as a result of it, please do let us know, at **bookend@TheNetworkEffect.co.uk**